STUDIES IN AMERICAN LITERATURE
Volume XIX

☆☆☆☆☆☆☆☆☆☆☆☆☆☆☆☆☆☆☆☆☆☆☆☆☆☆☆☆☆☆☆☆

SHOW THYSELF A MAN

A COMPARISON OF
BENJAMIN FRANKLIN AND COTTON MATHER

by

PHYLLIS FRANKLIN

1969

MOUTON

THE HAGUE · PARIS

LIBRARY OF CONGRESS CATALOG CARD NUMBER: 69-17876

Printed in The Netherlands by Mouton & Co., Printers, The Hague

For
Marie Margaret Bricker

PREFACE

The term *puritan* has had a rather unlucky history. It began in the sixteenth century as a word of derision and was still able, in the twentieth century, to arouse a negative response. When H. L. Mencken wrote, "Show me a Puritan and I'll show you a son-of-a-bitch", he expressed a fairly common attitude. His statement, coming so long after historical Puritanism had ceased to be a political or religious threat, shows the influence of more recent connotations attached to the word – associations which have grown out of the theories of Max Weber and Sigmund Freud or which more properly belonged to Victorianism. From the older negative concepts and the newer theories there evolved an image of the egotistic Puritan as a greedy hypocrite, suffering from repression, hysteria, and anal-eroticism.

Certainly the negative connotations of Puritanism have affected the reputations of both Cotton Mather and Benjamin Franklin. The stereotyped image of Mather reveals a hypocritical and hysterical Puritan while that of Franklin reveals a clever man who mouthed Puritan morality for profit. This study has grown, in part, out of the belief that Mather was less and Franklin more a Puritan than has been generally supposed and that their lives and writings reveal the inadequacy of the traditional Puritan image. I am grateful for the comments of Mrs. Juel Janis and Professor James E. Wellington. And I am particularly indebted to both Professor Robert S. Ward and Professor Clark M. Emery.

The University of Miami
June 1966

CONTENTS

I

A WORTHLESS FAITH

"A *Workless Faith* is a *Worthless Faith*".[1]

"No other man in America", wrote Vernon L. Parrington of Benjamin Franklin, "and few in Europe had so completely freed themselves from the prejudice of custom. The Calvinism in which he was bred left not the slightest trace upon him...".[2] To Parrington Calvinism denoted all that was un-American and illiberal, all that Benjamin Franklin, the first ambassador of American democracy, could not possibly represent. Calvinism was the "reactionary theology" of men like Cotton Mather, a theology that at the butt end of its days stood opposed to Franklin's "liberal political philosophy". Therefore, Parrington had no difficulty differentiating between Franklin, the liberal, and Mather, the reactionary. Benjamin Franklin, a kindly gray-haired wit and philosopher, had charming manners and an open mind; Cotton Mather, oversexed and overwrought, had forever spying eyes, a nose keen for his own publicity, and a crooked, diseased mind. While Franklin was unpretentious, Mather's egoism and lust for power blotted out his charity. Study might make Franklin rich in learning, but it only clogged Mather's mind. When Franklin became interested in science, it was a mark of breeding; when Mather "dabbled" in science, he listened with greedy avidity to old wives' tales. Whereas Franklin, ripe in the wisdom of this

---

[1] Cotton Mather, *Bonifacius: An Essay Upon the Good That is to be Devised and Designed* (Boston, B. Green, 1710), p. 37. Microcard. Hereafter designated *Essays to Do Good.*
[2] *Main Currents in American Thought* (New York, Harcourt, Brace & World, Inc., 1954), v. 1, p. 167.

world, was resourceful, discreet, competent, and an early and faithful friend to principles of federation, Mather groveled, padded his bibliography like a college professor, distorted facts to suit his fantastic perspective, blundered through worldly affairs, scolded like a fishwife, dripped with devil-talk and sodden morality, and contained not a grain of liberalism in his entire make-up.[3]

When Parrington placed Franklin and Mather in their neat and opposing pigeonholes, he neglected to consider a letter written by Franklin to Cotton Mather's son, Samuel.

Permit me to mention one little instance, which, though it relates to myself, will not be quite uninteresting to you. When I was a boy, I met with a book, entitled 'Essays to do Good', which I think was written by your father. It had been so little regarded by a former possessor, that several leaves of it were torn out; but the remainder gave me such a turn of thinking, as to have an influence on my conduct through life; for I have always set a greater value on the character of a *doer of good*, than on any other kind of reputation; and if I have been, as you seem to think, a useful citizen, the public owes the advantage of it to that book.[4]

Did Parrington ever wonder how a dribbling devil-talker like Mather could influence a man as sane and practical as Benjamin Franklin, a man whose main fault, according to Parrington, was his sharp spiritual limitation?

Although Parrington thought the letter not important enough to mention, it disturbed other Franklin students. E. E. Hale was certain that no one but Franklin "would have dared" to relate Franklin to Mather,[5] for everyone knew that Mather was an "ass" while Franklin was a "most useful practical genius".[6] James Parton thought it "exceedingly strange" that the influential book *Essays to Do Good* "should have been written by the man who, in 1692, at Salem, when nineteen people were hanged, and one pressed to death for witchcraft, appeared among the crowd, openly

---

[3] *Ibid., see* pp. 107-118 on Mather, pp. 166-181 on Franklin.

[4] *The Writings of Benjamin Franklin*, ed. by Albert H. Smyth (New York, The Macmillan Company, 1907), v. 9, p. 208. Hereafter designated Smyth ed.

[5] "What Made Benjamin Franklin?", *Christian Examiner*, 66 : 267 (March 1859).

[6] *Ibid.*, p. 274.

exulting in the spectacle!" [7] And Carl Van Doren some 74 years later still thought it "unexpected" that Franklin had apparently borrowed an idea from Cotton Mather.[8]

Eventually a few critics concluded that the "Protestant Ethic" of Puritanism had marked Franklin as well as Mather. A. W. Griswold believed that "While Cotton Mather represents the mind of orthodox Puritanism, . . . Franklin [represents] a secularized version of the same." [9] The editors of the 1964 edition of *The Autobiography* make a similar statement: "Though Franklin rejected Mather's theology, he retained the Puritan social conscience. . . . In a non-moral way Franklin 'perceived that the Puritan virtues had immense utilitarian value'." [10]

Because Mather has traditionally represented America's villains while Franklin generally is listed in American hagiology, few critics have seriously considered the possibility of Mather's influence upon Franklin. Underlying their evasion of a Mather-Franklin relationship has always been a basic assumption that the two men were different.

It is now more than 300 years since Mather was born and 173 years since Franklin died, a sufficient lapse of time, one would think, to permit this question to be studied without the traditional prejudices surrounding Calvinism and Puritanism – and Cotton Mather. Were Franklin and Mather alike or different? Can the traditional position represented by Parrington be justified? Replacing the two men in their respective corners to gather dust in dignified opposition will not be difficult, but we may find that a new examination will return them to the same side of the literary historian's shelf. For when their lives and writings are studied without bias and in terms of their own works rather than

---

[7] *Life and Times of Benjamin Franklin* (New York, Mason Brothers, 1864), v. 1, p. 47.

[8] *Benjamin Franklin* (New York, The Viking Press, 1938), p. 75.

[9] "Three Puritans on Prosperity: Cotton Mather, Benjamin Franklin, and Timothy Dwight", *New England Quarterly*, 7 : 489 (Summer 1934).

[10] Leonard W. Labaree *et al.* (eds.), "Introduction", *The Autobiography* (New Haven, Yale University Press, 1964), p. 18. Hereafter designated *Autobiography*. Partially quotes Griswold, "Three Puritans on Prosperity", *New England Quarterly*, 7 : 488 (1934).

works about them, one important concept held in common emerges
– a belief that man is improvable. Whether or not Mather influenced Franklin is not the present question, for the belief that
man may exert himself in his own behalf seems to be rooted in
their common background, New England Puritanism.

But the brand of Puritanism they shared was not exactly that
of the founders of Massachusetts. Although there had never
been a point in time when the old beliefs were formally denied,
there had been a subtle but revolutionary movement from emphasis upon justification by faith to justification by faith *and
works*. This revolution could occur quietly because the new Puritanism "was not enacted in the sphere of ideas, it did not challenge creeds or raise doctrinal heresies – it was staged in the heart
and among the affections, and stressed old morals in new ways".[11]
New England Puritanism as it emerges from Perry Miller's studies
had the formlessness of an amoeba. Its protaplasm contained
imbalances, which reacted to outer stimulation by spreading for-
ward first in one direction and then in another until, unaware of
what was happening, it found itself in a new position. The economic, social, and political changes in Europe and New England
provided the stimulus.

The founders of the Massachusetts Bay Colony belonged to
that Puritanism most narrowly defined as a reform movement
within the Church of England. But this is far too simple a defini-
tion, for they were also distinguished from other Puritans by their
general acceptance of congregational church polity, Ramist logic,
and federalist theory.[12] And even this is an inadequate description,
for they brought with them to the new world a cosmic view of
God and man which was at once of the Middle Ages and of the
Renaissance; which expressed both a "mood of mysticism" [13] and
a reliance upon intellect; which conceived of man as debased and
sinful and yet exalted his reason. For them, God could be omni-

---

[11]   Perry Miller, *The New England Mind from Colony to Province* (Cambridge, Harvard University Press, 1953), pp. 409-410.
[12]   Perry Miller, *The New England Mind: The Seventeenth Century* (Cambridge, Harvard University Press, 1954), p. 374.
[13]   Max Savelle, *Seeds of Liberty* (New York, A. A. Knopf, 1948), p. 23.

potent and man could have free will; He would damn because He was just and save because He was merciful. This precarious balance of concepts, which Miller considers the true Puritanism of the founders, gave way when the New Englanders tried to defend their theology against the attacks of Roman Catholics, Arminians, and Antinomians and still maintain a theological position that neither Cromwell, Charles or James II could attack.

Changes occurred slowly during the seventeenth century as theologians dissected and elaborated upon the process of regeneration. Originally they had conceived of man as passive, waiting for an infusion of grace that would make him feel as one with the creator and sustainer of the universe, and enable him to act in accordance with God's will. He was helpless in the knowledge that "grace [was] a supernatural power and that no man [could] enact regeneration by his own exertions".[14]

From this conception of a passive man, waiting on God's pleasure, there grew up a belief in an active man who could Prepare himself for salvation. Congregationalism was at least partially responsible for the change in position, for a church made up of visible saints required a means for recognizing those eligible for membership. The Puritans had gone beyond Augustine when they tried to discern the "signes of Faith" that could separate the saints from the sinners in this life, and the need for determining an elect led to an acceptance of external signs of regeneration. As time went on, pressures from England made it desirable that church membership be more easily available, and there was also a local need for enough saints to maintain church government. As a result, the desire for church membership and the power "to take up the church covenant ... became presumptive proof of experience, and a workable basis for the order".[15]

Along with the emphasis on external proof for church membership (which made no pretense of representing assured sainthood), there evolved, as the covenant theology developed, a belief that "Preparation" was a preliminary phase of regeneration. In this phase, "preliminary motions" would be experienced that

---

[14] Miller, *The New England Mind: The Seventeenth Century*, p. 27.
[15] Miller, *The New England Mind from Colony to Province*, p. 69.

would "sooner or later ... eventuate in conversion".[16] Because
the covenant theology was stated so often in contractual terms,
the element of chance in receiving grace seemed to diminish. God
had freely bound himself to fulfill certain conditions if man in
his turn would keep the covenant. Preparation came more and
more to represent man's part of the agreement. In *The Day of
Doom* (1662), Michael Wigglesworth had stated the older position when he portrayed God as saying:

> Am I alone of what's my own,
>   no Master or no Lord?
> And if I am, how can you claim
>   what I to some afford?
> Will you demand Grace at my hand,
>   and challenge what is mine?
> Will you teach me whom to set free,
>   and thus my Grace confine? [17]

Increase Mather, in 1710, clearly expressed the shift in emphasis:

We never dare say, ... that if men improve their natural abilities,
grace will infallibly follow ... still, 'there will not one Sinner in all
the Reprobate World, stand forth at the Day of Judgment, and say,
Lord, Thou knowest I did all that possibly I could do, for the obtaining Grace, and for all that, Thou didst withhold it from me'.[18]

Increase Mather did not deny the older concept. He paid lip service with "We never dare say", and then went on to elaborate the
new position.

The concept of a passive and helpless man was modified by
the new emphasis upon a God bound to honor a man's earnest
Preparation. Cotton Mather advised men to " 'Try whether you
can't give that Consent; if you can, 'tis done!' " [19] He would not
accept inability as an excuse for not trying. Men, he wrote, "fear-
fully abuse the Doctrine of Man's Inability to turn to God and
walk with Him, until supernatural Grace enable him, as if it were

---

16   *Ibid.*, p. 55.
17   Michael Wigglesworth, *The Day of Doom* (New York, American News
Company, 1867), CLXXIX, p. 72.
18   Miller, *The New England Mind from Colony to Province*, pp. 409-410.
19   *Ibid.*, p. 67.

a very pretty Apology for their Continuance in their Slothfulness and Wickedness".[20] Quite clearly, then, he did not advocate
helpless waiting; instead he encouraged men to begin the process
by their own endeavors. He did not think of himself as initiating
a new approach – he was only elaborating standard doctrine. On
Judgment Day man was to plead faith first, and then, to show
that his faith was not that of a hypocrite, he was to plead, "It was
a Faith which disposed me to all the Good Works of thy Holy
Religion. . . . Thus [Mather concluded] you have *Paul* and *James*
Reconciled. Thus you have *Good Works* provided for." [21]

As Preparation received greater emphasis, methods for Preparation became of greater interest, and in order to determine the success of his efforts man looked in the only direction he could – to
external signs. The "signes of Faith" might at least be tentatively
identified by the desire and ability to join in the church covenant;
they could also be determined by the doing of public good. "True
Piety", said the Rev. Dr. William Cooper, "as it will not let Men
live to a bad end, so it can't but make them to live to some good
end; and none are so Publicly Useful, such Universal Blessings as
are the Pious and Godly." [22]

Miller thinks that the course of New England Puritanism was
firmly set in the direction of Arminianism in 1637 with the resolution of the "Antinomian Controversy", when Anne Hutchinson
was defeated, for "all the argument with Mrs. Hutchinson
[boiled] down to her denial that . . . [Preparation as] a phase of
conversion [existed]".[23] In Cotton Mather, Miller sees "The cul-
minations of this development", and rates *Essays to Do Good* (the
book that Franklin stated had influenced him), as "possibly the
most important work in the early eighteenth century", for it clearly
expressed the concept of Practical Piety, the new spirit of Puritan-

---

[20] *Diary of Cotton Mather*, ed. by Worthington Chauncey Ford (= *Massachusetts Historical Society Collections*, Seventh Series (Boston, Published
by the Society, 1911), v. 7, p. 573. Hereafter v. 7 designated *Diary*, 1, and
v. 8, *Diary*, 2.
[21] *Essays to Do Good*, p. 37.
[22] Miller, *The New England Mind from Colony to Province*, p. 414.
[23] *Ibid.*, p. 57.

ism in which man attempted to improve himself and then to improve his society.[24]

By citing Cotton Mather as an exponent of Practical Piety, Miller disposes of part of the myth that labeled Mather an "orthodox" Puritan. It seems worth a momentary digression to examine briefly other questionable aspects of the Mather myth.

In 1907, George Lyman Kittredge studied the events leading up to the Salem Witchcraft trials. "The . . . outbreak", he pointed out, "was not due to Puritanism", or to a peculiarity in the New England temper, nor was it a "sign of exceptional bigotry or abnormal superstition".[25] To believe in the possibility of witches was no more superstitious than to believe in the possibility of God. There is no doubt that Cotton Mather believed in witches – he was a good Christian of the seventeenth century, and he further intended to make use of the manifestations "to Confound the *Sadducism* and *Atheism* of a debauched Age".[26] There is equally little doubt that if he had had his way the accused witches might have endured no more than the prayers of those godly enough to fast and pray for them.[27] Unable to prevent the executions, he did his best to warn against the use of spectral evidence, but again,

[24] *Ibid.*, p. 410.
[25] "Notes on Witchcraft", *Proceedings of the American Antiquarian Society* (Worcester, Mass., Published by the Society, 1907), v. 18, p. 163.
[26] Samuel Mather, *The Life of the Very Reverend and Learned Cotton Mather* (Boston, 1729), p. 46.
[27] In a letter dated 31d 3m 1692, written to John Richards, one of the judges at the Salem trials and a member of Mather's congregation, Mather suggested "it is worth considering, whether there be a necessity alwayes by Extirpacons by Halter or fagott, [   ] every wretched creature, that shall be hooked into some degrees of Witchcraft. What if some of the lesser Criminalls, be onely scourged with lesser punishments, & also put upon some solemn, open, Publike & Explicit/renunciation of the Divil? I am apt to thinke that the Divels would then cease afflicting the neighbourhood whom these wretches haue 'stoo'd (?) them vpon, . . . Or what if the death of some of the offenders were either diverted or inflicted, according to the successe of such their renunciation" (*Mather Papers*, notes by Rev. Thomas Prince, ed. by T. C. Robbins, H. W. Torrey, and S. K. Lothrop, Massachusetts Historical Society Collections, Fourth Series, Boston, Published by the Society, 1868, v. 8, p. 396, ed's. brackets). His diary entry for May, some two weeks before writing the letter to Richards, records, "In this *Evil-Time*, I offered, at the beginning, that if the *possessed* People, might bee scattered far asunder, I would singly provide for six of them;

his advice was not taken.[28] Despite Parton's dramatic statement, there is no sound evidence that he was responsible for or even took pleasure in the events at Salem in 1692.

And there is less reason for considering him a political reactionary. Clifford K. Shipton has pointed out that in overthrowing Governor Andros the clergy "were fighting for something more than the regaining of . . . political importance . . ." for "it was not until some time after the revolution that Massachusetts decided to go back to the old form of government, and no less a person than Calef [Mather's enemy] is the authority for the statement that Cotton Mather and some of the other ministers were the chief

---

and wee would see whether without more bitter methods, *Prayer* with *Fasting* would not putt an End unto these heavy Trials: But my offer (which none of my Revilers, would have been so courageous or so charitable, as to have made) was not accepted" (*Diary*, 1, pp. 151-152).
[28] In a letter to John Richards, dated May 31, 1692, Mather wrote, ". . . I must most humbly beg you that in the Managemt of the affair in your most worthy hands, you do not lay more stresse vpon pure Spectre testimony then it will bear". "It is very certaine that the divells have sometimes reprsented the shapes of persons not onely innocent, but also very vertuous" (*Mather Papers*, p. 293). On June 15, 1692, the Ministers of Boston drew up a statement of their position in regard to the witchcraft trials. Mather was not only one of the signers, but "drew it up" (*Diary*, 1, p. 151). "We judge that in the prosecution of these, and all such Witchcrafts, there is need of a very critical and exquisite Caution, lest by too much Credulity for things received only upon the Devil's Authority, there be a Door opened for a long Train of miserable Consequences, . . . IV. As in Complaints upon Witchcrafts, there may be Matters of Enquiry, which do not amount unto Matters of Presumption, and there may be Matters of Presumption which yet may not be reckoned Matters of *Conviction*; so 'tis necessary that all Proceedings thereabout be managed with an exceeding tenderness towards those that may be complained of; . . . V. When the first Enquiry is made into the Circumstances of such as may lie under any just Suspicion of Witchcrafts, we could wish that there may be admitted as little as is possible, of such Noise, Company, and Openness, as may too hastily expose them that are examined: . . . VI. Presumptions whereupon Persons may be committed, and much more Convictions, whereupon Persons may be condemned as guilty of Witchcrafts, ought certainly to be more considerable, than barely the accused Persons being represented by a Spectre unto the Afflicted; . . ." (reprinted in Kenneth B. Murdock, *Increase Mather*, Cambridge, Harvard University Press, 1925, Appendix B, pp. 405-406).

opponents of that step".[29] If power alone had been Mather's ambition, he would not have opposed the theocracy, nor would he have turned down the opportunity to be Rector of Yale College.[30]

With the new spirit of Practical Piety, he tried to lead his more conservative parishioners toward a fuller acceptance of the Half-Way covenant. He advocated the reform of church singing, and he was part of the group that drew up the Proposals of 1705 – a group "engaged in a struggle to bring their churches to a gentler and more liberal Calvinism".[31] He corresponded with and admired the Pietist, A. H. Francke, who sought church unity through an emphasis upon the practical aspects of Christianity in order to avoid doctrinal disputes.[32] When the Brattle Street Church was founded it was he who "helped . . . draw up an agreement whereby all four Churches in Boston could live in harmony" [33]; and he could boast in *The Wonders of the Invisible World* that for the New England Churches, "the Names of *Congregational, Presbyterian, Episcopalian,* or *Antipoedo-baptist,* are swallowed up in that of *Christians*".[34]

His scientific writings represent far more than an avidity for old wives' tales. *The Angel of Bethesda,* his medical treatise, reveals extensive medical knowledge and was, in fact, the "first general treatise on medicine written in the English colonies in America". Mather may not have practised medicine formally, but he shared theories held by the "most progressive medical students of his day".[35] He was responsible for introducing smallpox inoculation in America; he inclined toward the acceptance of the idea

[29]   "The New England Clergy", *Publications of the Colonial Society of Massachusetts* (Boston, Published by the Society, 1937), v. 32, p. 29.

[30]   Kenneth Murdock, "Cotton Mather and the Rectorship of Yale College", *Publications of the Colonial Society of Massachusetts* (Boston, Published by the Society, 1927), v. 26, p. 401.

[31]   Shipton, p. 31.

[32]   E. Benz, "Ecumenical relations between Boston puritanism and German pietism: Cotton Mather and August Hermann Francke", *Harvard Theological Review,* 54 : 171 (July 1961).

[33]   Ralph and Louise Boas, *Cotton Mather* (Hamden, Connecticut, Archon Books, 1964), p. 135.

[34]   Reprint, Mount Vernon, New York, n.d.

[35]   Daniel J. Boorstin, *The Americans* (New York, Random House, 1958), pp. 222-223.

of an "animal machine" in which "disease was caused by the malfunctioning of the mechanical parts"; and he looked for particular remedies for particular diseases.[36] He was aware that mental attitudes could influence physical health and the treatment he advocated for the mentally ill was surprisingly humane for his day.[37] Otho Beall and Richard Shyrock consider that Mather's significance in medicine lies in his "open-mindedness" as well as in his "ability to select out of contemporary science certain ideas which were to prove of lasting value".[38]

Mather's scientific interests extended beyond the medical field. His book *The Christian Philosopher* represented "the first extensive use of Newtonian ideas in the American colonies",[39] and also revealed him as a student of botany and zoology as well as astronomy. This book and the rest of the *Curiosa Americana* show Mather to be "the foremost American gatherer and disseminator of the new scientific knowledge during his time".[40]

In 1958, Daniel Boorstin noted that "sober scholarship has lately begun to divest Mather of his Mephistophelian character", so that he might one day be fully rescued from "the ill-informed hatred of generations of liberal historians".[41] Actually, as early as 1940, Perry Miller, who has since done more than his share in propounding the Mather myth, noted that Mather's *Manuductio Ad Ministerium* showed "how far he had travelled with that segment of Puritanism that was journeying toward Arminianism, morality, and Unitarianism, that segment of which Benjamin Franklin was an offshoot, and against which Jonathan Edwards fought in his endeavor to revivify the seventeenth century spirit".[42]

---

[36] O. T. Beall and Richard H. Shyrock, "Cotton Mather: First Significant Figure in American Medicine", *Proceedings of the American Antiquarian Society* (Worcester, Mass., Published by the Society, 1954), v. 63, pp. 64-66.
[37] *Ibid.*, p. 112.
[38] *Ibid.*, p. 132.
[39] Theodore Hornberger, "Notes on the Christian Philosopher", in Thomas J. Holmes, *Cotton Mather: A Bibliography of His Works* (Cambridge, Harvard University Press, 1940), v. 1, p. 136. Hereafter designated *Bibliography*.
[40] Beall and Shyrock, p. 112.
[41] *The Americans*, p. 221.
[42] *Bibliography*, v. 2, pp. 634-635.

Unfortunately, Miller's comment is entombed in Thomas J. Holmes' excellent but lengthy bibliography of Mather's works. In 1964, Richard Hofstadter, in *Anti-intellectualism in American Life*, specifically named Cotton Mather as one of the enlightened Puritan clergymen

who were cosmopolitan in outlook, relatively liberal in religious tendency, and conversant with the latest intellectual influences from Europe. . . . Such influence as they had they used to encourage greater tolerance, a broader pursuit of learning, the cultivation of science, and the restraint of some of the bigoted tendencies of the leading country laymen, the public, and the less enlightened clergy.[43]

Parrington had not believed that Mather belonged in any way to the American tradition, but Parrington had not begun to understand Cotton Mather. He never realized that in Mather's zeal for Practical Piety, the balanced Puritanism of the founders had given way: the Renaissance had replaced the Middle Ages; reason had all but overwhelmed mysticism; and the structure of the earth and its creatures had been recognized as wonderfully contrived despite the damage they had incurred in man's fall.

For the first seventeen years of his life Benjamin Franklin lived in Boston where the ideas of the new Puritanism mixed quietly with the older dogmas. Franklin may have shaken the dust of Boston from his shoes when he sailed for New York, but he never was free from its spirit.

[43]   Richard Hofstadter, *Anti-intellectualism in American Life* (New York, Alfred A. Knopf, 1963), pp. 62-63.

II

A DOER OF GOOD

> For I have always set a greater value on the character
> of a doer of good, than on any other kind of repu-
> tation.[1]

The new Puritanism that Cotton Mather represented and which
Franklin claimed had influenced him was founded upon the
belief that man could exert himself in his own behalf and, in so
doing, would work for the good of others. Over the years Mather
had tried to develop a method men could follow in attaining
Practical Piety, and the *Manuductio Ad Ministerium*, written two
years before his death, outlines the course he recommended for
others and had followed himself. It is interesting to note how
closely Franklin's efforts paralleled Mather's.

Mather asserted that man might improve himself in two steps.
First, one made Preparation for receiving grace; [2] then, he methodically went about "... Shunning every thing that the Light of GOD
in you shall condemn as an *Evil Thing*: and in filling your Life
with Acts of Devotion towards GOD. ..." [3] He provided a series of
questions as a guide toward the accomplishment of this Devotion.
The first consideration was, "*What shall I do for MY SELF, that
I May MY SELF Improve in Knowledge and Goodness: and*

---

[1] Benjamin Franklin, "To Samuel Mather", *The Writings of Benjamin
Franklin*, ed. by Albert H. Smyth (New York, The Macmillan Company,
1907), v. 9, p. 208. Hereafter designated Smyth ed.
[2] *Manuductio Ad Ministerium* (Boston, 1726), pp. 16-20, Microfilm.
I have reproduced all 's's in modern form and omitted the single quotation
mark where it was not functional. Hereafter designated *Manuductio*.
[3] *Ibid.*, p. 19.

the Ends of those Means, which the Divine Cultivation employs upon me?" [4]

Mather's efforts to improve in knowledge began early for he had, according to Peabody, a "passion for books and learning" and "his studies in preparation for college were more extensive, than was usual at that day".[5] He had the benefit of the best formal education colonial America offered but continued his studies afterwards during his seven years as tutor [6] and throughout an unusually active career. He taught himself French, Spanish, "and in his Forty-fifth Year . . . Iroquois Indian . . .".[7] He owned a library of "7000 or 8000 Volumes of the most curious and chosen Authors" considered "by far the most valuable Part of the family Property".[8] He advised those who had spare time to *"Give thy self unto Reading.* Good BOOKS of all Sorts, may employ your Liesure, and Enrich you with Treasures more valuable than those, which the way and Work of your Callings would have purchased." [9] He claimed, and his contemporaries supported his claim, that "Seldome any *new Book* of Consequence finds the way from beyond-Sea, to these Parts of *America,* but I bestow the Perusal upon it".[10]

Franklin, despite a limited formal education (less than one year in the Grammar School plus some time in "a School for Writing and Arithmetic"),[11] gained through his own study

[4] *Ibid.,* p. 21.
[5] William B. O. Peabody, "Life of Cotton Mather", *The Library of American Biography,* ed. by Jared Sparks (Boston, Hilliard, Gray & Co., 1836), v. 6, pp. 171-172.
[6] Samuel Mather, *The Life of the Very Reverend and Learned Cotton Mather* (Boston, 1729), p. 40.
[7] *Ibid.,* p. 49.
[8] Daniel J. Boorstin, *The Americans* (N.Y., Random House, 1958), p. 298.
[9] *Bonifacius, An Essay Upon the Good that is to be Devised and Designed* (Boston, B. Green, 1710), p. 50. Microcard. Hereafter designated *Essays to Do Good.*
[10] *Diary of Cotton Mather,* ed. by Worthington Chauncey Ford (= *Massachusetts Historical Society Collections,* Seventh Series) (Boston, Published by the Society, 1911), v. 7, p. 548. Hereafter v. 7 designated *Diary,* 1, and v. 8, *Diary,* 2.
[11] Benjamin Franklin, *The Autobiography,* ed. by Leonard W. Labaree *et al.* (New Haven, Yale University Press, 1964), p. 53. Hereafter designated *Autobiography.*

enough knowledge to make him feel at home with the intellectuals of America, England, and France. His studies, like Mather's, began early and were deliberately directed toward improving his writing and language, his skill at "Figures", his knowledge of Rhetoric and Logic and the Socratic method of dispute.[12] When he was twenty-seven he began to study languages: French, Italian, Spanish, and Latin.[13] Throughout his career as printer, politician, scientist, and ambassador, he continued to study, buying books and reading in all fields except "Religious Controversy".[14]

Mather had considered that a man's first effort at self-improvement was to increase in knowledge, his second was to increase in goodness. In the *Essays to Do Good,* Mather had suggested that "every man *Devise* what *Good* may be done, for the Help of what is yet Amiss, in his own heart and Life".[15] One must "Enquire not only, *What we have done,* but also, *What we* have to do? Frequent Self-Examination is to find out, the Points, wherein we are to Amend our wayes." He recommended the writing down of resolutions and looking them over at suitable intervals "to see how far you have Proceeded in the Execution of them".[16]

Mather's personal practice followed his precept. According to his son Samuel, he had been impressed when he was fifteen with the importance "of proceeding *Methodically* in this *great Duty* of *Christianity*". His method for self-improvement involved "*first,* an *Examination* of himself, *next,* an *Expostulation* with himself; and *last,* a *Resolution . . .*".[17] In his series of daily questions aimed at Serviceableness, he asked on Saturday, "*What more have I to do for the Interest of GOD in my own Heart and Life?*"[18] Every morning Mather thought of and recorded "the Devices of Good" to be done.[19] He aimed at control of particular

---

[12] *Ibid.,* pp. 62-64.
[13] *Ibid.,* p. 168.
[14] Benjamin Franklin, *To William Strahan* (= *The Papers of Benjamin Franklin,* ed. by Leonard W. Labaree *et al.,* New Haven, Yale University Press, 1959, v. 2, p. 411. Hereafter designated as Yale ed.
[15] *Essays to Do Good,* p. 43.
[16] *Essays to Do Good,* pp. 41-44.
[17] Samuel Mather, p. 8.
[18] *Ibid.,* p. 59.
[19] *Diary,* 2, p. 23.

traits, resolving "to watch and pray, against *Lascivious* Thoughts, *ambitious* Thoughts, and *wandring* Thoughts in the Times of Devotion",[20] and to govern his pride:

Concerning my PRIDE, I examined myself, by all the Discoveries of it; but I found especially two Respects, wherein I was most wofully guilty before the Lord.

First, my *Applauding* of myself in my Thoughts, when I have done any Thing at all significant. ... *Proud Thoughts* fly-blow my best Performances! [21]

His *Diaries* list his temptations, his failures, and his progress at improving himself. But he found that recording all activities was too difficult and his last entry for 1705/6 registers this objection:

God never required or expressed any such thing of any man that he should Register every occurrence of his Life. For such an Attempt were to justle out more necessary and important Duties. Upon this and many other accounts, it is both unwarrantable and Impertinent.[22]

In *Poor Richard* for 1749 Franklin noted that "many pitch on no course of life at all, nor form any scheme of living, by which to attain any valuable end; but wander perpetually from one thing to another".[23] His own scheme for attaining a valuable end was then about 23 years old. During the voyage from London to Philadelphia in 1726, he had conceived of a *"Plan* . . . for regulating my future Conduct in Life. It is the more remarkable, as being form'd when I was so young, and yet being pretty faithfully adhered to quite thro' to old Age." [24]

Franklin's plan was very like Mather's in spirit. Cataloguing thirteen virtues, he attempted to master them one by one, keeping written records of his progress and observing a "daily Examination" combined with a Prayer. At the same time, "The Precept of *Order* requiring that *every Part of my Business should have its allotted Time"*, he planned his day. Rising at five, he was to ask himself, "The Morning Question, What Good shall I do this

---

20   *Ibid.*, 1, pp. 3-4.
21   *Ibid.*, p. 16.
22   *Ibid.*, p. 544.
23   Yale ed., v. 3, p. 341.
24   *Autobiography*, p. 106.

Day?" and in the evening, "What Good have I done to day?" His
experience in keeping records was rather like Mather's, for, "After
a while I went thro' one Course only in a Year, and afterwards
only one in several Years, till at length I omitted them entirely,
being employ'd in Voyages and Business abroad with a Multiplicity
of Affairs, that interfered, but I always carried my little Book with
me." [25] Like Mather, he had difficulty in maintaining goodness.
At least he admits to failure in achieving Order and avoiding
Pride, "the *last* vice the good man gets clear of".[26]

Neither Mather nor Franklin was content to limit self-improvement to self-effort. Mather had believed that self-improvement
could be promoted through clubs. In the *Manuductio*, he advised
students:

Form a SODALITY. What I mean, is, Prevail with a Fit Number, [*Six*
or *Seven* may be a Competency, or Fewer, if you can't find so many,]
of Sober, Ingenious, and Industrious Young Men, to Associate with
you, and meet *One Evening* in a *Week*, for the spending of Two or
Three Hours, in a *Profitable Conversation.* . . .[27]

The questions he proposed related to the studies of the young men,
and Mather concluded that as a benefit the group consideration
would be,

. . . a way to clench the *Nails* that have been struck into your Minds;
and a Compendious and Charitable Course to come at the *Wealth*
which the *Diligence* of your Brethren has made them the Owners of;
together with the *generous Pleasure* of making them the Partakers of
yours. 'Twill have a Tendency also to qualify you for *Useful Con-
ference* in *other Company.* . . .[28]

Mather himself had experienced the benefits of such a club, for
he had belonged "to a *Society of Young Men that met on the
Sabbath Evening* for Religious Ends and Purposes; and unto
these Meetings he ascribed his *first* Rise and Improvement in the
Art of *Speaking,* of *Praying,* &c".[29]

Franklin initiated a society of young men for similar reasons.

25   *Ibid.*, pp. 151-155.
26   "Poor Richard", 1749, Yale ed., v. 3, pp. 343-344.
27   *Manuductio*, pp. 72-73. Mather's brackets.
28   *Ibid.*, pp. 73-74.
29   Samuel Mather, p. 7.

In the Autumn of 1727, he "... form'd ... a Club for mutual Improvement..." – the well known Junto. The members were to suggest "... Queries on any Point of Morals, Politics or Natural Philosophy", and to write and read Essays.[30] There were "Standing Queries" [31] to be asked at each meeting, some of which were aimed at improvement of the individual's knowledge and goodness. The first question was designed to improve the members' knowledge "particularly in history, morality, poetry, physic, travels, mechanic arts, or other parts of knowledge". Other questions were directed at moral improvement: "What unhappy effects of intemperance have you lately observed or heard? of imprudence? of passion? or of any other vice or folly?", and "What happy effects of Temperance? of prudence? of moderation? or of any other virtue?" "Do you know of any fellow citizen, who has lately done a worthy action, deserving praise and imitation? or who has committed an error proper for us to be warned against and avoid?" Physical improvement was considered too – "Have you or any of your acquaintance been lately sick or wounded? If so, what remedies were used, and what were their effects?" [32] Other questions were directed at convenience ("Who do you know that are shortly going voyages or journies, if one should have occasion to send by them?") and mutual assistance or protection ("Hath any body attacked your reputation lately? and what can the Junto do towards securing it?"; "Is there any man whose friendship you want, and which the Junto or any of them, can procure for you?"; "Have you lately heard any member's character attacked, and how have you defended it?"; "Hath any man injured you, from whom it is in the power of the Junto to procure redress?"; "In what manner can the Junto, or any of them, assist you in any of your honourable designs?"; and "Have you any weighty affair in hand, in which you think the advice of the Junto may be of service?" [33]

---

[30] *Autobiography*, **pp.** 116-117.
[31] These Queries are not believed to be the original ones, but are assigned to the year 1732. *See* "Standing Queries for the Junto", Yale ed., v. 1, pp. 255-256.
[32] *Ibid.*, **p.** 257.
[33] *Ibid.*, **pp.** 257-258.

The final part of Mather's first suggestion for self-improvement called for the fulfillment of *"the Ends of those Means*, which the Divine Cultivation employs upon me". Man strove for goodness and knowledge not because they possessed abstract value, but because they enabled him to better fulfill whatever tasks God placed upon him. Mather performed not only the normal duties of his calling as minister, but also stopped to consider each Sabbath morning, *"what Service to be done for my Saviour, in the* FLOCK *whereof I am the Pastor"*.[34] So seriously did he regard his obligation to his congregation that he fasted privately for each member requesting "the most suitable Blessings for them".[35] In order to fulfill his own calling, he tried to bring other men to realize their callings. "To Spread the Nets of Salvation for men, in the ways of their *Personal Callings,* and convey Good Though[ts] unto them, in the *Terms* and *Steps* of their Daily Business, is a Real Service to Interests of Piety." [36] The Sodality's function was to provide a means for the young candidates of the ministry to improve in those talents necessary for their calling.

Franklin's society had a similar function. Among the Junto questions were three specifically aimed at worldly advancement: "Hath any citizen in your knowledge failed in his business lately, and what have you heard of the cause?"; "Have you lately heard of any citizen's thriving well, and by what means?"; "Have you lately heard how any present rich man, here or elsewhere, got his estate?" [37]

Business success alone, however, was not Franklin's goal. He accepted responsibility as a printer, excluding "all Libelling and Personal Abuse", and noted unhappily that many printers were not only not averse to using scandal but were also

so indiscreet as to print scurrilous Reflections on the Government of neighbouring States, and even on the Conduct of our best national Allies, which may be attended with the most pernicious Consequences.[38]

---

[34]   *Diary,* 2, p. 24.
[35]   Samuel Mather, p. 39.
[36]   *Essays to Do Good,* p. 178.
[37]   "Standing Queries for the Junto", Yale ed., v. 1, p. 257.
[38]   *Autobiography,* p. 165.

He apparently agreed with Mather that

> If you *Terminate* in an *Inferior* End, and rise no Higher in your Aims, than to have your SELF accommodated with such Things as a *Carnal Mind* calls, *Comfortable Circumstances.* Your *Life*, what is it but a perpetual Folly. . . .[39]

And so at age forty-two, he retired, content with a "sufficient tho' moderate Fortune", which freed him for scientific study and public service.[40]

Implicit in Mather's and Franklin's desire to improve in virtue *and* in knowledge was the belief that such improvement was not only possible but was necessary for the fulfillment of man's duty to God. Christianity had recognized a religious calling; Calvinism extended the religious calling to secular activity. In New England in the first half of the seventeenth century John Cotton had preached that "faith draws the heart of a Christian to live in some warrantable calling".[41] A man has been given gifts for his calling by God and after a calling is determined, "then he depends upon God for the quickening and sharpening of his gifts in that calling".[42] The new spirit of Puritanism made man try to help himself and others in the "quickening and sharpening" instead of depending solely upon God.

This desire to quicken and sharpen one's gifts in a calling was at least partially the reason for Mather's founding the Sodality and Franklin's founding the Junto. But both men expressed their belief in the importance of a calling in other ways too. Franklin wrote in "The Way to Wealth", *"He that hath a Trade hath an Estate*, and *He that hath a Calling hath an Office of Profit and Honour*; but then the *Trade* must be worked at, and the *Calling* well followed. . . ."[43] Mather said in the *Manuductio*, "You must be *Diligent in your Business* if you would hope to stand in any Desireable Circumstances *before* that Great KING,

[39]   *Manuductio*, p. 5.
[40]   *Autobiography*, p. 196.
[41]   John Cotton, "Christian Calling", *The American Puritans*, ed. by Perry Miller (Garden City, New York, Doubleday Anchor Books, 1956), p. 173.
[42]   *Ibid.*, p. 175.
[43]   Yale ed., v. 7, p. 342.

unto whose Holy Service you are Dedicated." And he reminded his readers that the Service of God required "*a Workman that need not be ashamed*".[44]

Naturally, both men praised industry. Franklin listed it as one of his thirteen virtues, and Mather wrote "There never was an *Eminent*, who was not an *Industrious* Man." [45]

Because the work of a calling was performed in a material world, Franklin and Mather were concerned with those aspects of worldly living that might influence man's efforts. Like Calvin, they were interested in the effects of both food and drink. Mather had advised, "What of the *Table*, may for Quality or Quantity, indispose me for Thy *Work*, I will for *that Cause* avoid it." [46] Like Franklin, who had from his youth experimented with a vegetarian diet and later in life prided himself on the small amounts of simple food that could sustain him, Mather believed, "Indeed, if less *Flesh* were eaten, and more of the *Vegetable* and *Farinaceous* Food were used, it were better." [47] He advised, "*Don't eat too much!*" [48] and concluded that

The *Grand Secret* and *Sole Method* for *Long Life*, and so for the *Health* which will befriend and sweeten it, is, To keep the *Blood* and *Juices* in a State of due *Fluidity*. And nothing will do this, but keeping much to a *Spare, Lean, Fluid* sort of a *Diet*. All who *live long*, and without much *Pain*, and after such a Life at length *Die easily*, are such as Live *Abstemiously*.[49]

Aware of the effect food and drink could have on one's work, Franklin had attempted to reform his fellow printers of "their muddling breakfast" of strong beer.[50] Later he listed temperance on his roster of virtues; "Eat not to Dulness. Drink not to Elevation." [51] Planning for the students at the Academy, he recommended that they "diet together, plainly, temperately, and frugal-

---

[44] *Manuductio*, pp. 26-27.
[45] *Ibid.*, p. 27.
[46] *Manuductio*, p. 12.
[47] *Ibid.*, p. 132.
[48] *Ibid.*, p. 136.
[49] *Ibid.*, p. 130.
[50] *Autobiography*, pp. 99-101.
[51] *Ibid.*, p. 149.

ly".[52] The 1742 edition of *Poor Richard* placed special emphasis on rules of health. "If thou eatest so much as makes thee unfit for Study, or other Business, thou exceedest the due Measure." Not only was the "exact Quantity" of food and drink necessary for the "Services of the Mind" but there was added incentive: "A sober Diet makes a Man die without Pain; it maintains the Senses in Vigour; it mitigates the Violence of Passions and Affections." [53]

The desire for moderation in the enjoyment of sensuous pleasures is perhaps best expressed in Franklin's attitude toward drinking. As early as 1722, using the name Silence Dogood, he asked, "What Pleasure can the Drunkard have in the Reflection, that, while in his Cups, he retain'd only the Shape of a Man, and acted the Part of a Beast." [54] In 1732, he remarked in *The Pennsylvania Gazette*, while describing the death of an alcoholic, "who ever heard of a Sot reclaim'd? If there are any such they are Miracles".[55] Compiling "The Drinkers Dictionary", (1737) he concluded,

... I was even tempted to add a new one my self under the Letter B, to wit, *Brutify'd*: But upon Consideration I fear'd being guilty of Injustice to the Brute Creation, if I represented Drunkenness as a beastly Vice, since, 'tis well-known, that the Brutes are in general a very sober sort of People.[56]

But though drunkenness was bad, moderate drinking was enjoyable. The Junto queries were to "be read distinctly each Meeting [with] a Pause between each while one might fill and drink a Glass of Wine".[57] Perhaps the happiest expressions of his enjoyment of wine are represented in the drinking songs he composed.[58] Franklin agreed with Increase Mather that "drink is itself 'a good

---

[52] "Proposals Relating to the Education of Youth in Pennsylvania", Yale ed., v. 3, p. 402.
[53] *Ibid.*, v. 2, pp. 339-341.
[54] *The New England Courant*, No. 12, Sept. 10, 1722, *ibid.*, v. 1, p. 40.
[55] *Ibid.*, p. 278.
[56] *Ibid.*, v. 2, pp. 177-178.
[57] "Proposals and Queries to be Asked the Junto", *ibid.*, v. 1, p. 259.
[58] *See* "The Antediluvians Were All Very Sober", Yale ed., v. 3, p. 52.

creature' to be received with thankfulness, 'the wine is from God, but the Drunkard is from the Devil' ".[59]

Moderation was important to both men, not only as a sign of grace, for "Faith frames the heart to moderation",[60] but also because it improved man's health and so better enabled him to fulfill his obligation to God.

Both men were aware that living successfully in the world required a certain amount of self-discipline, and for that reason they respected similar virtues. Franklin had listed as his second virtue, "Speak not but what may benefit others or yourself. Avoid trifling Conversation",[61] and added, "Speak little, do much." [62] Mather said that one should not "*Tell all he knows*"; and further advised, "*Think* before you *Speak; Think* before *whom* you Speak; Think *why* as well as *what* you Speak. . . . And, *Least said soonest mended.*" [63] Franklin, despite his lengthy public career, spoke infrequently, and then was described as saying only what was necessary.[64] Mather, too, perhaps originally because of his stammering, adopted a deliberation in his manner of speaking,[65] choosing to "studiously decline to utter anything, that I may foresee, will be *useless*, and much more, every Thing that may bee *hurtful*, and *sinful*, to bee uttered".[66]

They believed that man should waste neither words nor money. Mather advised that "One must not *Spend all he hath*",[67] and Franklin listed frugality as a virtue. But he did not advocate the saving of gold for its own sake:

If I knew a miser, who gave up every kind of comfortable living, áll the pleasure of doing good to others, all the esteem of his fellow-citizens, and the joys of benevolent friendship, for the sake of accu-

---

[59] Perry Miller, *New England Mind: The Seventeenth Century* (Cambridge, Harvard University Press, 1954), p. 42.
[60] John Cotton, "Christian Calling", p. 179.
[61] *Autobiography*, p. 149.
[62] Yale ed., v. 5, p. 471.
[63] *Manuductio*, pp. 137-138.
[64] Carl Van Doren, *Benjamin Franklin* (New York, The Viking Press, 1938), pp. 529-530.
[65] Samuel Mather, p. 20.
[66] *Diary*, 1, p. 207.
[67] *Manuductio*, p. 137.

mulating wealth, *Poor man,* said I, *you pay too much for your whistle.*[68]

Frugal of words and money, they were also wary of wasting time. Thomas J. Holmes has pointed out that "Both Cotton and Increase Mather were outstanding among those pioneers who early taught the infant nation to value time, elevating the principle into religion." [69] Mather had written that man should spend his time "in such a Manner, as is most worthy of a reasonable Creature".[70] He warned that controversy would only "Divert the *Studies* . . . from such things as would be much more Profitable for your self and others".[71] Franklin had refused to take the time to defend his electrical experiments. Like the Mathers he valued time:

> Some sweet Employ for leisure Minutes
> chuse,
> And let your very Pleasures have their
> Use.
> But if you read, your Books with Prudence
> chuse.
> Or Time mis-spent is worse than what you
> lose.[72]

Man was to make the best use he could of his time, his money and his abilities, and he must not be sidetracked into forgetting the purpose of his calling. One should "go on to *do as well as you can*, what you have to do. Let not the *Crooked Things that can't be made streight*, encumber you." [73] Franklin, too, had reminded himself to "Be not disturbed at Trifles, or at Accidents common or unavoidable." [74]

Franklin concluded his list of virtues with humility – "imitate Jesus and Socrates".[75] Mather advised that "While you are yet in

[68] "The Whistle", Smyth ed., v. 7, pp. 415-416.
[69] *Cotton Mather: A Bibliography of His Works* (Cambridge, Harvard University Press, 1940), v. 2, p. 485. Hereafter designated *Bibliography.*
[70] *Diary,* 2, p. 133.
[71] *Manuductio,* p. 141.
[72] "Poor Richard", 1752, Yale ed., v. 4, p. 88.
[73] *Manuductio,* p. 147.
[74] *Autobiography,* p. 150.
[75] *Ibid.*

your *Younger Years*, be always furnished with a Stock of Weighty and Useful *Questions*", and added, "whenever you are *Arguing*, ordinarily propose every Thing rather *Socratically* than *Dogmatically*".[76] As a young man Franklin had recognized the value of the Socratic method and used it successfully in both Boston and Philadelphia.[77]

All of these bits of practical advice were based on a belief that moderate pleasure was both reasonable and beneficial for man. To Franklin Reason equalled Virtue, Virtue Reason, and "Virtue and Happiness are Mother and Daughter." [78] To Mather, "the Law of *Reason* . . . [was] the Law of God; . . . Our submission to the Rules of *Reason* is an Obedience to God",[79] and such obedience would ultimately lead to man's greatest happiness. In "The Busy-Body" Franklin had written.

. . . it is certainly of more Consequence to a Man that he has learnt to govern his Passions; in spite of Temptation to be just in his Dealings, to be Temperate in his Pleasures, to support himself with Fortitude under his Misfortunes, to behave with Prudence in all Affairs and in every Circumstance of Life; I say, it is of much more real Advantage to him to be thus qualified, than to be a Master of all the Arts and Sciences in the World beside.[80]

As a second step in one's Dedication to God or practice of piety, Mather had advised considering means for helping one's relatives. He asked each Monday morning, "*what to be done in* MY FAMILY", and on alternate Tuesdays, considered "*what Service to be done for Christ, and my* RELATIVES ABROAD?" [81] As one might expect he was concerned for the salvation of his children's souls, and particularly sorrowed as his son Increase seemed less and less likely to be saved.[82]

He also considered carefully his children's education and surroundings, planning that they "shall have their Apartments well-

[76]   *Manuductio*, p. 143.
[77]   *Autobiography*, pp. 65, 88.
[78]   "Poor Richard", 1746, Yale ed., v. 3, p. 64.
[79]   *Diary*, 2, p. 144.
[80]   No. 3, Yale ed., v. 1, p. 119.
[81]   *Diary*, 2, pp. 25-26.
[82]   *Ibid.*, pp. 528-529.

fitted up, in which they may read, and write, and pray".[83] He devised rules of conduct for them, especially for "Cressy".[84] He believed that children should be expert readers and write "a fair Hand",[85] and further,

that among all the Points of a Polite Education [w]h[i]c[h] I would endeavour for my *Children*, they may each of them, the *Daughters* as well as the Sons, have so much Insight into some ski[ll], which lies in the way of Gain . . .[86].

He wanted his daughters to be prepared for housekeeping,[87] to write well and to be skilled at shorthand.[88] His daughter Katherine learned Latin, Hebrew, and medicine, [89] and was probably the first female to receive medical training in America.[90] He made the dinner table a pleasant place for instructive stories [91] and tried to think of "monitory and profitable" sentences whenever he would see the children during the day.[92]

He tried to form in his children a spirit of "Benignity" toward one another,[93] and refrained from striking them "except it be for an atrocious Crime or for a lesser Fault Obstinately persisted in".[94] Boas points out that Mather's "views of discipline, education, and parenthood were such as to place him among the most enlightened of present day educators".[95] Samuel Mather recalls that his father had charmed his children.[96]

Mather extended his help, both spiritual and practical, to those

[83] *Ibid.*, p. 25.
[84] *Ibid.*, p. 389.
[85] *Essays to Do Good*, p. 58.
[86] *Ibid.*, p. 63.
[87] *Diary*, 2, p. 51.
[88] *Ibid.*, pp. 43-44.
[89] Boorstin, p. 187.
[90] O. H. Beall and R. H. Shyrock, "Cotton Mather: First Significant Figure in American Medicine", *Proceedings of the American Antiquarian Society* (Worcester, Mass., Published by the Society, 1954), v. 63, p. 56.
[91] *Diary*, 2, p. 262.
[92] *Diary*, 1, pp. 534-535.
[93] *Ibid.*
[94] *Essays to Do Good*, pp. 59-60.
[95] Ralph and Louise Boas, *Cotton Mather* (Hamden, Connecticut, Archon Books, 1964), pp. 252-253.
[96] Samuel Mather, p. 140.

beyond his immediate family – to nephews, sisters, and his wives' relatives.

We know much less of Franklin's family life. We do know that he encouraged his daughter Sarah to attend church services,[97] and that he was interested in the kinds of education his children and grandchildren received. Like Mather, he believed that a practical education "which lies in the way of Gain" would be helpful for women.[98] He had advised against a foreign education for his grandson William Bache, suggesting instead that the boy learn French, mathematics, and "a knowledge of Accounts", in America.[99] He sent his grandson, Benjamin Bache, to school in Geneva, "As I intend him for a Presbyterian as well as a republican." [100] He, too, believed that a "Fair handwriting" was important and he registered an objection to stays for young girls.[101]

He was most generous with financial help, providing for his sister Jane Mecom and aiding her son Benjamin. He helped his brother James' son and widow, and his brother Peter's widow. A. H. Smyth noted that

Franklin's first official act was to appoint his son controller of the post-office. The postmastership of Philadelphia he gave first to his son, then to Joseph Read, one of his wife's relatives, then to his own brother. Indeed, there were few of the Franklins, Reads, and Folgers who did not profit by their thrifty and energetic kinsman's zeal for the public service. He looked after them all: brothers, and cousins, and nephews, and brothers-in-law drew salutary incomes from public offices.[102]

Mather's third step in the Dedication to God required an inquiry into "the several SOCIETIES to which you stand related" as the church, the town and the land. "Think, *What Good is to be proposed and promoted here!*" [103] His question for Wednesday mornings was "*what Service to be done for Christ, and the Interest of*

---

97   "To Sarah Franklin", Smyth ed., v. 4, p. 287.
98   *Autobiography*, p. 166.
99   "To Richard Bache", Smyth ed., v. 8, p. 305.
100 "To Mrs. Sarah Bache", *ibid.*, v. 7, p. 348.
101 "To Mrs. Mary Hewson", *ibid.*, v. 8, p. 426.
102 "The Life of Benjamin Franklin", *ibid.*, v. 10, p. 173.
103 *Manuductio*, pp. 21-22.

His Kingdome, in the Countrey, or among other People?" "*. . . The Kingdome of God* in the World, Calls for Innumerable Services from us.*" Men who devised means for promoting either spiritual or temporal good would fulfill this step in the achievement of practical piety.[104] Reason alone had brought even a very wicked writer to conclude that,

To Love the Publick, to Study an Universal Good, and to Promote the Interest of the Whole World, as far as is in our Power, is surely the Highest of Goodness, and makes that Temper, which we call Divine.[105]

The goal of the *Essays to Do Good* was to encourage ". . . *Brethren to Dwell together in Unity,* and carry on every Good Design with United Endeavours",[106] for man was "a Sociable Creature".[107] With this principle in mind, Mather had formed in Boston the Neighborhood Benefit Societies and devised ten questions to be considered at each meeting. These questions were directed at public improvement and show a concern for maintaining peace and order, serving "the Interests of Religion", fighting ". . . Ignorance and Wickedness", opposing ". . . Oppression or Fraudulence", influencing legislation, and aiding those "under sore and sad Affliction".[108]

He also formed a Society for the Propagation of the Christian Religion,[109] several religious societies for young men,[110] and "projected a *Society of Peacemakers* . . . whose Business it was to compose and prevent Differences, and divert Lawsuits that might arise".[111] He had been a member of America's first scientific

---

104　*Essays to Do Good*, p. 20.
105　*Ibid.*, p. 22.
106　"Preface", *ibid.*, p. iv.
107　*Methods and Motives for* SOCIETIES *to Suppress Disorders* (Boston, Printed by B. Green and J. Allen?, 1703), p. 1, in *Bibliography*, v. 2, p. 679.
108　James Parton, *Life and Times of Benjamin Franklin* (New York, Mason Brothers, 1864), v. 1, p. 48.
109　*Diary*, 1, pp. 418-419.
110　*Ibid.*, 2, p. 44.
111　Samuel Mather, p. 48.

society, founded in 1683 by his father,[112] as well as a member of the Royal Society.

It has generally been recognized that Franklin patterned the Junto after Mather's plans for the Neighbourhood Benefit Societies.[113] The purpose of the Junto was twofold, for along with mutual improvement, the members were to consider, "any thing at present, in which the Junto may be serviceable to *mankind,* to their country, to their friends, or to themselves". They considered whether "any deserving stranger . . ." or "any deserving young beginner lately set up" might need help. They tried to improve their land by asking "Have you lately observed any defect in the laws of your *country*, [of] which it would be proper to move the legislature for an amendment? Or do you know of any beneficial law that is wanting? . . . Have you lately observed any encroachment on the just liberties of the people?" [114]

Franklin was also a member of the Royal Society, the Society for the Encouragement of Arts, Manufactures and Commerce, and the founder of a philosophical society.

In fact, almost all of his efforts toward serving the public were accomplished through "united Endeavours". In the *Essays to Do Good*, Mather had pointed out that though a person were of *"Low Degree"* he could still hope to do good, for "It is possible the *Wisdom of a Poor man,* may Start a Proposal, that may *Save a*

---

[112] O. T. Beall, "Cotton Mather's early 'Curiosa Americana' ", *William and Mary Quarterly*, 18 : 361 (July 1961).

[113] James Parton assumed that Franklin learned of Mather's clubs as a child when he may have attended meetings with his father. Franklin may also have seen a copy of Mather's book, *Religious Societies* (Boston, 1724), on his brief visit to Boston in April or May of 1724. Sometime in April or May Franklin called upon Mather, who had received the copies of *Religious Societies* from the printer on March 31 (*Diary*, 2, p. 712). Since it was Mather's well-known custom to hand out his books of piety whenever he could, he may have given the young man a copy on that visit. If so, this might be a likelier and more immediate source for the Junto, established three years later, than childhood memories alone. In this book Mather described the organization and questioning procedures for his societies and listed a set of rules governing the topics to be discussed. A facsimile of the rules is reproduced in *Bibliography*, v. 2, p. 900.

[114] "Standing Queries for the Junto", Yale ed., v. 1, pp. 257-258. Ed's. brackets.

City, Serve a Nation!" [115] Franklin had tried to save a city by writing *Plain Truth,* and he did indeed Serve a Nation. Most of his efforts toward public improvement are too well known to need elaboration. He took part in founding a library,[116] a hospital, and a school. He was active in organizing firemen and policemen. He proposed plans "for the paving and the better cleaning and lighting of city streets".[117]

Like Mather he recognized that man was "a sociable being" [118] and conceived of a "Society of the Free and Easy", an organization made up of men who had achieved improvement in goodness by following his plan for self-improvement. Free from the dominion of vice, they were to help each other in worldly affairs and, as a group, work for the welfare of others.[119]

Both men recognized a relationship between economic security and the ability to do good. Aware that a rational man free from financial pressures could more easily achieve virtue, Franklin stressed the economic precepts with which he has become most closely associated. He seemed to believe firmly that a competence was the first step in freeing man from "Slavery to his Creditors." Only then could man transcend himself and party interests to do good for others.[120] Mather had objected to the "senseless Party-Spirit",[121] and was vaguely aware that a sufficient amount of money was necessary for a man to rise above private interests. He had personally suffered "many wants and Straits: in my Diet, much; in my Habit, more". He knew that financial pressure could "pull me back, and keep me low".[122]

Mather, too, conceived of men working in societies of "ani-

---

[115] P. 31.

[116] Franklin may have recalled that in *Essays to Do Good,* Mather had noted that "The Tradesmans Library needs to be more Enriched" (p. 178).

[117] Carl Becker, "Franklin, Benjamin", *Dictionary of American Biography* (New York, Charles Scribner's Sons, 1931), v. 6, p. 588.

[118] "Journal of a Voyage", Yale ed., v. 1, p. 85.

[119] *Autobiography,* pp. 162-163.

[120] Franklin had written, with obvious disdain, to Charles W. F. Dumas, that "Some writer, I forget who, says, that Holland is no longer *a Nation,* but *a great Shop;* and I begin to think it has no other Principles or Sentiments but those of a Shopkeeper" (Smyth ed., v. 8, p. 292).

[121] *Diary,* 2, p. 515.

[122] *Ibid.,* p. 630, also p. 703.

mated good Men".[123] Perhaps Franklin had recalled Mather's comment that,

The English Nation once had a Sect of men called, *Bonhommes*, or, *Good men*. The ambition of this Book, is to Revive and Enlarge a Sect, by the coming of *all men* into it.[124]

Again, in 1717, Mather had suggested that "SOCIETIES of Good Men" who had attained some degree of "PIETY" should work together to eliminate differences in religion, hoping "to become a *Great Mountain and fill the whole Earth*".[125]

Franklin accepted Mather's ideal of an organization of good men which would gradually include more and more men working for the public good. But he thought that man needed specific directions for attaining goodness and so he advocated that all those belonging to the Society of the Free and Easy should fulfill his plan for attaining virtue.

Many people lead bad lives that would gladly lead good ones, but know not *how* to make the change. They have frequently *resolved* and *endeavoured* it; but in vain, because their endeavours have not been properly conducted. To expect people to be good, to be just, to be temperate, &c., without *shewing* them *how* they should *become* so, seems like the ineffectual charity mentioned by the Apostle. . . . [126]

The instrument of his "art" was to be, for Christians, "a faith in Christ, as the effectual means of obtaining the change they desire". For those who had less faith, "the *Art of Virtue* may be of service", "but all may be more or less benefited by it".[127]

While Mather believed in group action, he also acted regularly as an individual in doing good. On Fridays he considered, *"what particular Objects of Compassion have I to do good unto?"* [128] Sometimes he gave spiritual aid by paying for the printing of "an Essay to advance Knowledge and Goodness among Children",[129]

123   *Ibid.*, 1, p. 500.
124   "Preface", *Essays to Do Good*, p. vii.
125   *Malachi*, 2nd ed. (Philadelphia, 1767), pp. 92-93, in *Bibliography*, v. 2, p. 597.
126   "To Lord Kames", Smyth ed., v. 4, pp. 12-13.
127   *Ibid.*, pp. 13-14.
128   *Diary*, 2, p. 27.
129   *Ibid.*, p. 7.

or a book directed to orphans – to those who were afflicted and to those who had estates and might help the poorer ones.[130] He constantly distributed "Books of Piety". He traveled to the Almshouse to preach because the poor and the old could not easily come to church,[131] and he gave needed books to young candidates for the ministry who could not afford to complete their own libraries.[132] He seemed to be ever on the watch for poor widows or promising students who were too poor to go to school. There were many he helped either with his own funds or by soliciting help from others.[133] He took it upon himself to keep his own home stocked with medical supplies for the poor and the sick, and he trained his daughter Katherine in the art of dispensing them. In this he was "more social-minded than were most of the physicians", for "the free dispensary would not appear in English-speaking cities until later in the century".[134] He apparently acquired a reputation for kindness, for a maid escaping from service "in a very vicious Family" sought refuge in the Mather household.[135]

Franklin also tried to do good as an individual, giving advice in his almanacs and newspapers, supplying his readers with medical information as well as moral and economic precepts, and, of course, amusement. He tried to give charity in such a way that it might continue to evoke good results, as his loan to Benjamin Webb was to do:

I send you herewith a Bill for Ten Louis d'ors. I do not pretend to *give* such a Sum; I only *lend* it to you. When you shall return to your Country with a good Character, you cannot fail of getting into some Business, that will in time enable you to pay all your Debts. In that Case, when you meet with another honest Man in similar Distress, you must pay me by lending this Sum to him; enjoining him to discharge the Debt by a like operation. . . . I hope it may thus go thro' many hands, before it meets with a Knave that will stop its Progress. This is a trick of mine for doing a deal of good with a little money.[136]

130 *Ibid.*, pp. 57-58.
131 *Ibid.*, 1, p. 178.
132 *Ibid.*, 2, p. 179.
133 *Ibid.*, pp. 187, 225.
134 Beall and Shyrock, p. 57.
135 *Diary*, 2, p. 396.
136 "To Benjamin Webb", Smyth ed., v. 9, p. 197.

The codicil to his will, leaving funds that might be used again and again, expresses a similar sentiment – doing good in such a way that more and more people might benefit from it.[137]

Mather believed that men should try to do good for their church, their town, and their land. He worked as conciliator in Sudbury,[138] Taunton,[139] Boston,[140] and other communities. Aware that the ministers were suffering from insufficient salaries, he wrote "A MONITORY LETTER *concerning the Maintainance of Able and Faithful Ministers*", a book designed not only to arouse the consciences of the church members but also to promote the endeavours of the ministers.[141] He realized that more practical aid was necessary, and we find him often sending "such Releefs as [he was] . . . able" to minsiters troubled by "distressing Poverty".[142] He printed a "Proposal for an Evangelical Treasury; the Design of which was to advance a Fund for bearing the Expence of *building* Churches in destitute Places, of distributing Books of Piety, of *relieving poor* Ministers &c".[143] Certainly he was not easily daunted, for he even attempted to convert a "French Priest, who is an Instructor to the Indians . . . to the Protestant Religion . . .".[144]

Franklin, despite the fact that he did not regularly attend church, gave financial support to churches of various sects and acted as a member of the board of directors for the meeting house built to accommodate itinerant preachers.

Both men were interested in general community improvement. In *Essays to Do Good*, Mather had recommended, "If there be any BASE Houses, which threaten to debauch, and Poison, and confound the Neighbourhood, Let your charity to your Neighbours, make you do all you can, for the suppression of them." [145] In January 1744, Franklin was a member of the Philadelphia Grand

---

137 "Franklin's Last Will and Testament", *ibid.*, v. 10, pp. 501-508.
138 *Diary*, 1, p. 270.
139 *Ibid.*, 2, p. 64.
140 *Ibid.*, 1, p. 332.
141 *Ibid.*, p. 351.
142 *Ibid.*, 2, p. 92.
143 Samuel Mather, p. 48.
144 *Diary*, 2, p. 554.
145 *Essays to Do Good*, p. 78.

Jury and took some part in composing the "Presentment" which is signed by the foreman but written in Franklin's handwriting.[146]

> The Grand Jury observe with great Concern the vast Number of Tipling Houses within this City, many of which they think are little better than Nurseries of Vice and Debauchery, and tend very much to encrease the Number of our Poor ... tending to destroy in the Minds of our Youth, all Sense of the Fear of God and the Religion of an Oath, owes its Increase in a great Measure to those disorderly Houses.[147]

To Mather, keeping this rule, "*As we have Opportunity, let us do Good unto all men, ...*" [148] made a man "A Publick Spirit", for "... Whatever contributes unto the *Welfare* of *Mankind*, ... also is to *Glorify* [God]." [149] In January 1721/2, he noted a "fanciful and whimsical" idea – to write "on the Backs of the Bills [of credit] which come to me at any Time, ... some Text of Scripture, that shall have a Tendency, to awaken in the Minds of People, right Sentiments of this World, and of what is passing in it".[150] Franklin expressed a similar idea in a letter to Edward Bridgen:

> There had indeed been an intention to strike Copper Coin, that may not only be useful as small Change, but serve other purposes.
>
> Instead of repeating continually upon every halfpenny the dull story that everybody knows, (and what it would have been no loss to mankind if nobody had ever known), ... to put on one side, some important Proverb of Solomon, some pious moral, prudential or economical Precept, the frequent Inculcation of which, by seeing it every time one receives a piece of Money, might make an impression upon the mind, especially of young Persons, and tend to regulate the Conduct. ... [151]

Both men were drawn by the problems of the Negroes and the Indians. In the *India Christiana*, Mather speaks of a Happy Revolution – "*Then* should we see the Africans no longer treated like meer *Beasts* of Burden, as they are in the Plantations of cruel

---

146   Ed's. footnote, Yale ed., v. 3, p. 9.
147   "Presentment of the Philadelphia Grand Jury". *ibid.*, v. 3, p. 10.
148   "Preface", *Essays to Do Good*, p. v.
149   *Manuductio*, p. 8.
150   *Diary*, 2, p. 667.
151   Smyth ed., v. 7, pp. 381-382.

Americans." [152] In the *Essays to Do Good*, he wrote of "the *Slave Trade* . . . a Spectacle that Shocks *Humanity*". He expressed the idea poetically:

> *The harmless Natives basely they trepan,*
> *And barter Baubles for the Souls of men.*
> *The Wretches they to Christian climes*
> > *bring o'er*
> *To serve worse Heathens than they did*
> > *before.*[153]

Although he had owned slaves at various times,[154] he was concerned for their welfare and wondered if their treatment might not be "one thing for which our God may have a Controversy with us".[155] He aided a group of Negroes who had asked his help in "erecting . . . a *Meeting* for the Welfare of their miserable Nation that were Servants among us".[156] He supported a "*Charity-Schole*" for the instruction of Negroes and Indians,[157] composed an "IN-DIAN PRIMER" in 1699/1700,[158] and wrote a pamphlet objecting to the sale of liquor to the Indians.[159] He was concerned when he thought the Indians were being oppressed by the English [160] and published an Abstract of the "Lawes of the Province against punishable Wickedness", in their language.[161]

Franklin, too, had owned slaves and advertised their sale in his paper, but in the last years of his life he worked for the abolition of slavery. He wrote a satire attacking the slave trade and in a pamphlet described favorably the practices of the American In-

---

[152] In E. Benz, "Ecumenical Relations Between Boston Puritanism and German Pietism: Cotton Mather and August Hermann Francke", *Harvard Theological Review*, 54 : 86 (July '61).
[153] *Essays to Do Good*, pp. 58-59.
[154] Mather first learned of the practice of smallpox inoculation from a slave.
[155] *Diary*, 2, p. 687.
[156] *Ibid.*, 1, p. 176.
[157] *Ibid.*, 2, p. 500.
[158] *Ibid.*, 1, p. 328.
[159] *Ibid.*, pp. 342, 215.
[160] *Ibid.*, 2, p. 48.
[161] *Ibid.*, 1, p. 511. This language has been tentatively identified as Natick or Algonquin.

dians.[162] Like Mather, he was concerned when they were taken advantage of and vigorously objected to the outrage of the Paxton murder.

As an official or as a citizen, Franklin had worked for the improvement of his community and his country. Mather, too, was an active citizen, advocating that the "Bridewel [be put] into a good Condition", or that "Methods, for setting the Poor to work", be found, or initiating "a Town-Vote for the rectifying of gross Abuse in the Choice of Jurymen".[163]

He believed that one "must *come forth* to any *Publick Service* whereof you may be capable, when you are called unto it".[164] Though he had "always pressed *Peace* and *Love* and *Submission* unto a legal Government",[165] as did Franklin in the early period of difficulties with England, Mather reserved the right to criticize his government,[166] as Franklin had done; and when he thought it necessary, as he did during the Andros regime, he stepped in, playing an active part in a rebellion that could have cost him his life if the Glorious Revolution had failed. Like Franklin, he advocated action in rectifying government affairs, for,

The *Displacing of a Few Officers* on the Score of their being found Vicious Men would signify an hundred times as much to Mend the State of a Depraved, Betray'd, unprosperous Nation, as a Thousand *Proclamations against Vice* follow'd with no such Executions.[167]

They both agreed that the attitude of the administrators of government would determine the general condition of the people, for government "in the Hands of Men, Proud of Command, and bent to their own private Gain", will create "a miserable People".[168] Franklin had, of course, advocated that government positions not be sources of profit to ensure the services of only honorable men.

[162] *See* "On the Slave-Trade", Smyth ed., v. 10, pp. 86-91, and "Remarks Concerning the Savages of North-America", Smyth ed., v. 10, pp. 97-105.
[163] *Diary*, 1, pp. 422-423.
[164] *Essays to Do Good*, p. 151.
[165] Samuel Mather, p. 44.
[166] *Ibid.*, p. 47.
[167] *Essays to Do Good*, p. 122.
[168] *Ibid.*, p. 123.

They both conceived of government as protective – "A care of other Peoples Safety." [169]

Although the depreciation of the bills of credit had effected both men, they nevertheless agreed upon the necessity of a paper currency based on a commodity other than gold or silver. Mather took the side of those agitating for a land bank in what has been described as an issue drawn between the prosperous merchants and townspeople in the east and the less prosperous people from the country towns. In 1691, he wrote *Some Considerations on the Bills of Credit* and tried to arouse interest in England in the New Englanders' difficulties.[170]

Franklin, like Mather, favored an issue of paper money and wrote *A Modest Enquiry into the Nature and Necessity of a Paper Currency* to explain his position and arouse the public. Supporting the use of land as a security for paper currency, he pointed out that "as Bills issued upon Money Security are Money, so Bills issued upon Land, are in Effect *Coined Land*".[171]

In the *Essays to Do Good*, Mather had written that, "what is done for Schools, and for Coledges, and for Hospitals, is done for a *General Good*. *Endowing* of these, or the *Maintaining* of them, is, *at once* to Do Good unto many." [172] Franklin had done much "Good unto many" through his public activities, and Mather was equally zealous. Criticizing "the too general Want of Education",[173] he had worked for the establishment of charity schools as well as schools for Negroes and Indians. He sent gold to the East-Indies "for the Support of the charity-Schole at Malabar".[174] In 1685, he noted in his diary, "Never bee at Rest, while our Island here, the North part of *Boston*, is without a good *Schoolmaster*, and a florishing school." [175] In 1705/6 he published the proposals for "erecting and supporting, CHARITY SCHOOLS".[176] Again in

---

[169] *Ibid.*, p. 117. *Also see* "Plain Truth", Yale ed., v. 3, p. 199.
[170] *Diary*, 2, pp. 295-297.
[171] Yale ed., v. 1, p. 151.
[172] Pp. 147-148.
[173] *The Way to Prosperity* (Boston, 1690), pp. 33-34, from Samuel Morison, *Puritan Pronoas* (New York, New York University Press, 1936), p. 72.
[174] *Diary*, 2, p. 520.
[175] *Ibid.*, 1, p. 106.
[176] *Ibid.*, p. 530.

1709/10 he considered another plan for setting up a *"charity-School"*. By 1710/11 there were "three Charity Scholes" that needed additional financial aid.[177] During the next few years, he continued preaching and considering new plans for educating the poor, and when the "overstockt *Charity-Schole*" could not hold "some very poor" neighborhood children, he paid "for their Schooling" himself.[178]

He was also active in both New England colleges. On the Sabbath, he stoppped to ask himself what he could do in his position as Overseer of Harvard.[179] When he could he sent books both to Harvard and to Yale.[180]

Franklin, in addition to working with a group for the foundation of the Academy, acted as an individual in purchasing scientific equipment and giving books to Harvard.[181] He suggested to Thomas Hancock in 1755 a scheme for raising money for the Harvard Library.[182]

In the *Essays to Do Good*, Mather had proposed this question, *"How may I be a blessing in the World?* and, *what may I do, that Righteousness may more dwell in the World?"* [183] Franklin had projected good devices not only for his own land but for all people. Deeply concerned with the senseless brutality of war, but realistic enough to realize that complete abolishment of it was out of his hands, he tried, instead, to alleviate the effects on noncombatants. Throughout the Revolution he worked with his English friends for the exchange of prisoners and, when that failed, tried to ensure their better treatment. He thought in terms of a "Law of Nations" which would

protect, so that they should never be molested or interrupted by Enemies even in time of War; I mean Farmers, Fishermen, and Merchants, because their Employments are not only innocent, but

---

[177] *Ibid.*, 2, p. 45.
[178] *Diary*, 2, pp. 213-214.
[179] *Ibid.*, 1, p. 105.
[180] *Ibid.*, 2, p. 405.
[181] "To Thomas Hubbard", Smyth ed., v. 3, pp. 435-437.
[182] Yale ed., v. 6, p. 180.
[183] *Essays to Do Good*, p. 29.

for the common Subsistence and Benefit of the human Species in general.[184]

Disagreements among men were of so much less significance than man himself that they could be better settled "by Arbitration" or "even by the Cast of a Dye".[185] He thought, too, of a "Plan for Benefiting Distant Unprovided Countries".[186]

It was at least partially their desire to help mankind that led both Mather and Franklin to scientific studies. In Mather's opinion, man might strive not only for intellectual and moral improvement, but also for an alleviation of physical suffering. Despite the obstacles and confusion arising out of the debate over smallpox inoculation, he had kept records that were of great use to others. The statistics he recorded showed "that there was about nine times as much chance of death if one caught the smallpox in the ordinary course of infection as compared with the danger from inoculation".[187] Boorstin wrote:

The collection of these Boston statistics [were] a pioneer work in public health, one of the first cases of quantitative analysis of such a medical problem. They later proved significant, not only in establishing inoculation as a measure of preventive medicine, but as valuable raw material for the development of the 'calculus of probabilities' by mathematicians. . . . [188]

Mather had also tried to collect "effectual *Remedies* for all Diseases",[189] and during an epidemic of measles, published "a Letter about the *Right Management of the Sick under the Distemper of the Measles*".[190] His desire to help man avoid physical suffering led him to write his medical book.

Franklin had been interested in medicine, so interested that he wrote apologetically to his parents for his excessive "meddling in the Dr's Sphere".[191] Like Mather he was concerned about com-

[184] "To Messrs D. Wendorp and Thomas Hope Heyliger", Smyth ed., v. 8, p. 263.
[185] "To Mrs. Mary Hewson", *ibid.*, v. 9, p. 12.
[186] *Ibid.*, v. 5, pp. 340-344.
[187] Boorstin, p. 225.
[188] *Ibid.*
[189] *Diary*, 1, p. 163.
[190] *Ibid.*, 2, p. 272.
[191] "To Josiah and Abiah Franklin", Yale ed., v. 2, p. 413.

municable diseases, and when rumors arose after the death of his
son Francis that the boy had died as a result of inoculation,
Franklin published a statement explaining that the boy had not
been inoculated "but received the Distemper in the common
Way", and recommended inoculation.[192]

Mather's work in medicine had been of immediate practical
benefit to man, and there was much in Franklin's work that was
eminently practical – his studies in navigation, climate, agri-
culture, as well as his inventions such as the Pennsylvania fire-
place and the lightning rod. But the scientific interests of both
men extended beyond what might be considered as immediately
beneficial to man. They were interested in all aspects of the
rapidly developing science of their time. Like Richard Hofstadter's intellectual, they were "pledged, committed, enlisted" in
learning's cause and though they tried to use knowledge for man's
benefit, they thoroughly enjoyed the intellectual process.

However much they might have been drawn to scientific
studies because of their desire to do good or to satisfy curiosity's
demands, their motives were not at odds with the traditional Puritan interest in scientific study. The knowledge of God, according
to Calvin, was "exhibited without obscurity in the structure of the
world, and in all the creatures".[193] One was to know God not only
through His word, but also through His works.

Both men rejected metaphysics as unprofitable and advocated,
instead, a study of the natural world. Mather advised the candidates for the ministry to "Be sure, the *Experimental Philosophy*
is that in which alone your Mind can be at all established", for
"it may be, what is now most in vogue may anon be refuted and
refused like its Predecessors".[194] He warned against accepting
"Philosophical Romances" and suggested instead that they study
the "*Principles of* our *Perpetual Dictator*, the Incomparable Sr.

---

[192]   "The Pennsylvania Gazette", December 30, 1736, *ibid.*, p. 154.
[193]   John Calvin, *Institutes of the Christian Religion*, tr. and collated by
John Allen, 7th American Edition, Revised and Corrected (Philadelphia,
Presbyterian Board of Christian Education, n.d.), Bk. 1, 10.1.
[194]   This seems to be an early statement of the Pragmatist's position that
what is thought to be true today may not be thought true tomorrow.

Isaac Newton".[195] I. Bernard Cohen has placed Franklin's scientific work within the empirical Newtonian tradition of the *Optics*. The development of hypotheses that might be tested in experience was typical of Franklin's scientific work [196] as were his continual attempts "to unify all scientific explanations within a single comprehensive framework of material causes and conservation principles".[197] Franklin, like others within the Puritan tradition, believed that behind the complexity and seeming contradictions in God's works or word there was only one truth.

Learning, particularly scientific learning, then, was a means of knowing God "to repair the Ruins of our first Parents, [Franklin quotes Milton] by regaining to *know God aright*, and out of that Knowledge to *love him*, to *imitate him*, to be *like him*, as we may the nearest by possessing our Souls of true Virtue".[198] As man's confidence in his own ability increased, knowledge became more and more the connecting link between God and man. The study of the natural world helped man to know God and so to better glorify Him. Glorifying God and the *"Service of God, as some express themselves, is only the same Thing in other Words. For Doing Good to Men is the only Service of God* in our Power. . . ." [199] Mather had written, "I shall bee serviceable to God, in being serviceable to Man." [200]

And service does dominate each man's attitude toward science. They were anxious to disseminate any knowledge that might prove helpful, joining with others in societies for a more effective exchange of information. Their concern for helping man combined with their interest in speculation – permissible because it might increase man's knowledge of God's creation, and particularly in Mather's case, could also be used as a support for religion.

But both men, despite or because of the intellectual attractions

195 *Manuductio*, p. 50.
196 *Franklin and Newton* (Philadelphia, American Philosophical Society, 1956), p. 297.
197 *Ibid.*, p. 342.
198 John Milton, "Education", p. 373, in Franklin's "Education of Youth", Yale ed., v. 3, p. 419. *See* "Of Education", *The Works of John Milton* (New York, Columbia University Press, 1931), v. iv, p. 277.
199 "Education of Youth", *ibid.*
200 *Diary*, 1, p. 62.

of scientific study, found it necessary to establish limits. In *The Christian Philosopher*, Mather had quoted apparently from himself a passage he considered very important:

I am able to write in seven languages; I feast myself with the sweets of all the sciences, to which the more polite part of mankind ordinarily pretend. I am entertained with all kinds of histories, ancient and modern. I am no stranger to the curiosities, which by all sorts of learning are brought to the curious. Nevertheless, it appears to me more valuable than all this, it appears more delectable, it is a thing of a superior character, with a true spirit of charity, to relieve a poor, mean, miserable neighbour; much more to do any extensive service for the redress of those epidemical miseries, under which mankind in general is languishing, and to advance the kingdom of God in the world,[201]

Franklin, in a similar way, had advised Mary Stevenson that there was

a prudent Moderation to be used in Studies of this kind. . . . For there is no Rank in Natural Knowledge of equal Dignity and Importance with that of being a good Parent, a good Child, a good Husband or Wife, a good Neighbour or Friend, a good Subject or Citizen, that is, in short, a good Christian.[202]

He felt, that, "Had Newton been Pilot but of a single common Ship, the finest of his Discoveries would scarce have excus'd, or atton'd for his abandoning the Helm one Hour in Time of Danger. . . ." [203] The editors of the Franklin *Papers* point out the difference between Franklin's attitude in this instance and Thomas Jefferson's in a similar case. "In 1778 . . . [Jefferson] urged the astronomer David Rittenhouse to resume the scientific studies he had deserted for revolutionary politics, firmly declaring, 'No body can conceive that nature ever intended to throw away a Newton upon the occupations of a crown'." [204] For Mather and Franklin, scientific study was valuable, but man was even more valuable.

---

[201] Charlestown, Published at the Middlesex Bookstore, 1815, p. 299. Microfilm.
[202] "To Miss Mary Stevenson", Smyth ed., v. 4, p. 22.
[203] "To Cadwallader Colden", Yale ed., v. 4, p. 68.
[204] Julian P. Boyd and others (eds.), *The Papers of Thomas Jefferson* (Princeton, Princeton University Press, 1950), II, 203. In Yale ed., v. 4, p. 68.

Mather's final instruction for piety was that one "have a Time to think: *What Good lying out of my Reach may I see others capable of doing more than I?* And hereupon become an Humble Adviser unto them." [205] This had been very common practice for Mather. One of his most noteworthy endeavors grew out of his desire to help the struggling Connecticut college which later became a member of America's Ivy League. He decided to write to "a wealthy East-India merchant at London" for aid. His request to Elihu Yale was successful, and the Connecticut College received a new name and enough money to assure its continued existence.[206] Franklin thought in terms of doing good beyond his immediate reach, in the terms of his will, as wel as by passing on information, suggesting new ways for employing the poor [207] or the best way to plan a frontier settlement.[208]

Both men used the organizations they were involved in to extend their influence for doing good. Mather had attempted to establish many Neighbourhood Clubs and so extend his influence. Franklin enlarged the scope and influence of the Junto by having each of the original twelve members form a subsidiary club and act as its leader.[209]

Though all Christians were to love God first and then their neighbours as themselves, the desire to reach out as far as possible in doing good to others gained special significance in New England as the doing of public good became a sign of grace. The doctrine of the calling required men to live in a "warrantable calling", and to be warrantable, a calling must "not only aim at our own, but at the public good". Both Mather and Franklin had echoed John Cotton's earlier statement, "We live by faith in our vocations, in that faith in serving God, serves men, and in serving men, serves God." [210]

205   *Manuductio*, p. 22.
206   H. Bingham, "Elihu Yale Governor, Collector and Benefactor", *Proceedings of the American Antiquarian Society*, New series (Worcester, Mass., Published by the Society, 1938). v. 47, p. 132
207   Footnote, Yale ed., v. 5, p. 233.
208   "To Samuel Elbert", Smyth ed., v. 9. p. 626
909   *Autobiography*, pp. 170-171.
210   John Cotton, p. 176.

For Mather and Franklin, piety meant that man must try to help himself, and that as a result of his endeavors, he would help others and so glorify God. It was important to them that man learn how to improve himself, for if effort were possible, method could be vital. It is natural that those who believe man capable of improvement would be interested in formal education, as they both were. But their interest in education went beyond the mere establishment of places of learning. They were aware of the importance of the association of ideas and the development of habits. Mather, "in bringing up his children tried to make them believe that learning was a reward – a good thing rather than a punishment". Rather than have play serve as a reward for diligence, "He would have his Children account it a *Privilege* to be *taught*. ...." [211] He tried to keep "... Pennies, or Fruits, or Paints, proper to be bestow'd on little Children. And in the bestowing of them, I would alwayes endeavour to commend some Lesson of Piety, to be remembred, with them: and the more likely to be remembred, for the Token that accompanies them." [212] Franklin, too, believed that "*strong* and *lasting* Impressions" might be made "on the Memory of young Persons". [213] He noted that those students at the Academy who had already formed bad habits in reading were "rarely, with Difficulty, if ever cur'd, yet, when none have been already form'd, good ones are as easily learn'd as bad". [214]

Both men objected to punishment in teaching and preferred reward for things well done. Writing an elegy for Ezekiel Cheever, Mather suggested,

> Tutors, *Be* Strict; *But yet be* Gentle *too*,
> *Don't by fierce* Cruelties *fair* Hopes *undo*,
>
> . . . .
>
> *The Lads with* Honour *first and* Reason *Rule*;
> Blowes *are but for the* Refractory Fool. [215]

[211] Samuel Mather, p. 17.
[212] *Diary*, 2, p. 85.
[213] "Poor Richard", 1747, Yale ed., v. 3, p. 100.
[214] "Observations Relative to the Intentions of the Original Founders of the Academy in Philadelphia", Smyth ed., v. 10, p. 15.
[215] Elizabeth P. Gould, *Ezekiel Cheever, Schoolmaster* (Boston, 1904), p. 84, in S. E. Morison, *Puritan Pronoas*, p. 100.

In the *Essays to Do Good*, he advocated that discipline be maintained "with *Rewards*, as well as *Punishments*, . . . a Child of any Ingenuity, under the Expectations and Encouragements of being Rewarded, will do to the uttermost".[216] As a younger man, Franklin had objected to his brother's striking him, and as an adult, emphasized reward rather than punishment. In the "Constitutions of the Academy of Philadelphia", (1749) he had suggested that

THE Trustees shall in a Body, visit the Academy, once a Year extraordinary, to view and hear the Performances and Lectures of the Scholars, in such Modes, as their respective Masters shall think proper; and shall have Power, out of their Stock, to make Presents to the most meritorious Scholars, according to their several Deserts.[217]

In his will, he left "one hundred pounds sterling" to be used by Boston's free schools, so that the "interest annually shall be laid out in silver medals, and given as honourary rewards annually by the directors of the said free schools . . .".[218]

Franklin, in "Proposals Relating to the Education of Youth in Pensilvania", 1749, and Mather, in the *Manuductio,* showed their interest in formal instruction. Each prescribed a specific course of studies, recommended textbooks, and carefully considered the incidental values which students might gain from study. Like Locke, they were also concerned about their students' health.

Their mutual interest in improvement spilled over from self-improvement and public improvement to the promoting of formal learning. But even this was not enough to satisfy their appetite for teaching. Franklin had pointed out that Mather "was a man that never missed any occasion of giving instruction".[219] He might just as well have made the same statement about himself. One of the reasons – perhaps the sole reason – for writing the *Autobiography*, he said, was to supply a model that might be "fit to be imitated".[220] In the *Essays to Do Good*, Mather had suggested that one should consider the uses that might be made of "*former*

---

216   *Essays to Do Good*, p. 111.
217   Yale ed., v. 3, pp. 427-428.
218   Smyth ed., v. 10, p. 499.
219   "To Samuel Mather", *ibid.*, v. 9, p. 208.
220   *Autobiography*, p. 43.

Blemishes". "What Signal thing shall I do, to Save Others from Dishonouring the Great God by such Miscarriages, as I my self once fell into." [221] Certainly it was with just this spirit that Franklin enumerated his moral lapses or "errata", as he chose to call them, "errata" that later disturbed Parson Weems.

John Ross, studying the fictional characters Franklin created in the poor Richard almanacs, noted that at first there was a sharply drawn line between Franklin, the printer, who was to provide "useful" information, and Richard Saunders "the philomath with his wife, Bridget", who were to entertain. Ross says that little by little Franklin with his useful information overwhelmed the comic Richard until "The early Richard was finally submerged by the famous farewell preface of 1758, wherein a shadowy Richard appears, only to introduce the speech of a wise old man, Father Abraham, who . . . quotes *only* the shrewd, prudential maxims. . . ." [222]

Franklin considered the almanacs, as he did his newspaper, as vehicles of instruction.[223] Mather, too, had tried his hand at writing an almanac [224] and regularly used the press as a means for spreading his teachings. Their faith in instruction strongly influenced their style of writing. Since they wanted to appeal to reason, they, like other members of the Royal Society and like many Puritan divines of the seventeenth century, believed that clarity and brevity were essential. Mather desired to preach so that "People of the lowest Capacity and even *little Children* may take notice . . .".[225] Simplicity, however, was not enough, for ideas must be clothed so that they will be "sensible to the lowest and meanest Capacities, yea, to all *Flesh*, Thus to *seek out Acceptable Words*, would render you a most *Profitable* as well as *Agreeable Preacher*".[226] Franklin had noted, "If a Man would that his Writings have an Effect on the Generality of Readers, he

[221] *Essays to Do Good*, p. 49.
[222] "The Character of Poor Richard: Its Source and Alteration", *PMLA*, 55 : 793 (September 1940).
[223] *Autobiography*, p. 165.
[224] *The Boston Ephemeris*, 1683.
[225] *Diary*, 2, p. 215.
[226] *Manuductio*, p. 104.

had better imitate that Gentleman, who would use no Word in his Works that was not well understood by his Cook-maid." [227] He complimented Lord Kames on the *Introduction to the Art of Thinking*, because he had never seen "more solid, useful matter contained in so small a compass".[228] The words one used "should be the most expressive that the language affords, provided that they are the most generally understood". Because they were anxious to influence their readers, Mather and Franklin tried for clarity, the use of the most expressive words, and the compression of an idea into a short statement. Consequently they both made use of maxims and anecdotes.

Again, in their style of writing, they reflected the Puritan values of the Plain Style. The "virtues of style consisted primarily in the concreteness of phrase used in applications, in the speaking of truths so that the most simple and unlearned of auditors would comprehend them".[229]

Certain that man's duty lay in action, both Cotton Mather and Benjamin Franklin seriously undertook self-improvement and public improvement. The intensity of their devotion to helping others places them firmly in the New England tradition of Practical Piety. For them doing good was not occasional, it was a career that demanded constant thought. There seems to have been no part of their private or public lives (except for such errors as even saints are heir to) that was not founded upon the belief that man, a reasonable creature, could act in his own behalf, improving himself and then acting for the good of others. Both men would have heartily subscribed to this motto: "God helps those who help themselves."

[227] "On Literary Style", Yale ed., v. 1, p. 329.
[228] "To Lord Kames", Smyth ed., v. 4, p. 120.
[229] Miller, *The New England Mind: The Seventeenth Century*, p. 350.

III

TO PROVIDENCE, RESIGN THE REST

> Seek Virtue, and, of that possest,
> To Providence, resign the rest.[1]

Cotton Mather and Benjamin Franklin lived intensely active lives and they firmly believed that to live and work for one's self and the good of others fulfilled the highest purpose of man's existence. But though Mather had stressed the importance of works in his *Practical Piety*, he had never rejected the older Puritan dogmas. However much he urged men to Prepare themselves, however much he tried to ease past the problem of regeneration as God's free gift to man, he did not deny the necessity for grace. Before a man could hope to succeed in his practical efforts, "the Glorious *GOD of all Grace*, [must] give you a *New Heart*, and cause a *Regenerating Work* of His Grace to pass upon you".[2] Benjamin Franklin had been a wholehearted advocate of the secular aspects of Mather's Piety, but had he also been in agreement with Mather's religious beliefs?

Franklin's religion has not been easy to label. He is most often referred to as a Deist, but he has also been called a "Shaftesburian",[3] a "deistic fatalist", and a "Platonic polytheist",[4] as well

---

[1] Benjamin Franklin, "Poor Richard", 1740, *The Papers of Benjamin Franklin*, ed. by Leonard W. Labaree *et al.* (New Haven, Yale University Press, 1959), v. 2, p. 252. Hereafter designated Yale ed.

[2] Cotton Mather, *Manuductio Ad Ministerium* (Boston, 1726), p. 15. Microfilm. Hereafter designated *Manuductio*.

[3] A. O. Aldridge, "Franklin's 'Shaftesburian' Dialogues not Franklin's: A Revision of the Franklin Canon", *American Literature*, 21 : 154-155 (May, 1949).

[4] I. W. Riley, *American Philosophy* (New York, Russell & Russell, 1958?), p. 244.

as a "Pythagorean".[5] Some have believed he had "a vision, not unlike religion's",[6] or even that he was "deeply and thoroughly religious".[7] Others have called him an "ungodly Puritan",[8] an "out-and-out agnostic",[9] or "a disbeliever".[10] It is not surprising that critics have been confused when Dr. Joseph Priestley, a man whom Franklin called an "honest heretic",[11] lamented that Franklin had been "an unbeliever in Christianity".[12] An interesting statement, as James Parton has pointed out, since Priestley himself

rejected the doctrines of the Trinity, the Atonement, Original Sin, and Miraculous Inspiration ... regarded Jesus Christ as 'a mere man', but divinely comissioned and divinely assisted; and ... the Bible, he thought ... neither inspired, nor infallible, nor correct, and ... to be judged and criticised as other writings are. ... [13]

The varying estimations of Franklin's religion sometimes reflect a writer's personal attitudes but most often show a failure to recognize that Franklin's religion changed during his lifetime. His religious development is marked by three important changes which occurred roughly about 1721, 1726, and 1775.

His initial religious experience was that of New England Puritanism, for his father Josiah had been admitted to full communion in Boston's Old South Church. As the son of a member Franklin

---

[5] Bernard Fay, *Franklin: The Apostle of Modern Times* (Boston, Little, Brown and Company, 1929), pp. 91 and 117.

[6] Carl Van Doren, *Benjamin Franklin* (New York, The Viking Press, 1938), p. 182.

[7] Merton A. Christensen, "Franklin on the Hemphill Trial: Deism versus Presbyterian Orthodoxy", *William and Mary Quarterly*, 10 : 440 (1953).

[8] Harold A. Larrabee, "Poor Richard in an Age of Plenty", *Harpers Magazine*, 212 : 67 (January, 1956).

[9] A. W. Griswold, "Three Puritans on Prosperity: Cotton Mather, Benjamin Franklin and Timothy Dwight", *New England Quarterly*, 7 : 484 (Summer 1934).

[10] William C. Bruce, *Benjamin Franklin, Self-Revealed* (New York, G. P. Putnam's Sons, 1917), p. 82.

[11] "To Benjamin Vaughan", *The Writings of Benjamin Franklin*, ed. by Albert H. Smyth (New York, The Macmillan Company, 1907), v. 9, p. 677.

[12] Priestley, *Autobiography*, as quoted by James Parton, *Life and Times of Benjamin Franklin* (New York, Mason Brothers, 1864), v. 1, p. 546.

[13] *Ibid.*

had been baptised, had studied the Bible, and had listened to the sermons.

However, in 1721, influenced by the writings of Shaftesbury and Anthony Collins, he abandoned his father's religion and adopted Deism. He became skeptical of such dogmas as "the Eternal Decrees of God, Election, Reprobation, &c.",[14] he did not particularly value Revelation,[15] and rarely attended church.[16] He also became adept at logic and in 1725 revealed both his skepticism and his pleasure in rounding out a metaphysical argument in *A Dissertation on Liberty and Necessity, Pleasure and Pain.* Starting from the attributes of God, he argued to the conclusion that, because man did not have free will, he could not be held responsible for his actions, and that, though the soul might be immaterial and immortal, the individual soul, as such, ceased to exist after death and so would be unaware of its immortality.[17] Five years later he "wrote a piece on the other side of the question", proving that "all things are not ordained". He finally became disgusted with the uncertainty of "metaphysical reasonings" and gave them up for other studies "more satisfactory".[18]

The years from 1721, when he adopted Deism, to 1726, when his attitude toward religion began again to change, were years of travel and irresponsibility. A Deist at fifteen, a runaway apprentice at seventeen, at eighteen, he was stranded in London without family, friends, or money for a return passage. Ever since he had run away from Boston, he had managed to support himself, improve at his trade, and continue his studies. In America he had been flattered by the attentions of several governors, and in London he had come in contact with such men as Sir Hans Sloane, who was collecting "curiosities", Dr. Pemberton, who was then editing the third edition of Newton's *Principia*, and Dr. Bernard Mandeville, whose *Fable of the Bees* had impressed

---

[14] Benjamin Franklin, *The Autobiography*, ed. by Leonard W. Labaree *et al.* (New Haven, Yale University Press, 1964), p. 145. Hereafter designated *Autobiography*.
[15] *Ibid.*, p. 115.
[16] *Ibid.*, p. 147.
[17] Yale ed., v. 1, pp. 58-71.
[18] Benjamin Franklin, "To Benjamin Vaughan", Smyth ed., v. 7, p. 412.

London readers. Even so, he was still at twenty a good "Compostor" who had written a moderately interesting pamphlet – and nothing more.

In 1726, however, new prospects developed. Mr. Thomas Denham, a Philadelphia merchant living in London, offered to pay his passage to America and offered him a job as his clerk – a position that promised future prosperity. Franklin "immediately" accepted Mr. Denham's offer and left London in July 1726.

The voyage to America provided him with time to think about his new venture, and his journal records that he thought seriously about means of achieving success. Denham was a man whom Franklin later characterized as unusually honest and diligent; Franklin seems to have determined to become like him. Eight days after leaving London, he noted the "surprise" he felt at realizing that even such a man as the keeper of Carisbrooke Castle, a "silly old fellow", could correctly evaluate an important man's character, and he concluded,

... I believe it is impossible for a man, though he has all the cunning of a devil, to live and die a villain, and yet conceal it so well as to carry the name of an honest fellow to the grave with him, but some one by some accident or other shall discover him. Truth and sincerity have a certain distinguishing native lustre about them which cannot be perfectly counterfeited. ... [19]

He may have thought unhappily of his past behaviour – the abandonment of his apprenticeship, his conversion of Mr. Vernon's money, his unfair treatment of Deborah Read, and his attempted seduction of James Ralph's mistress. Certainly he clearly remembered these "errata" some forty-five years later when he wrote the first section of the *Autobiography*. He echoed the earlier journal entry when he described his rejection of metaphysical reasonings and his adoption of the belief "that *Truth, Sincerity and Integrity* in Dealings between Man and Man, were of the utmost Importance to the Felicity of Life ...".[20]

The plan for his conduct, which he felt was "Perhaps the most

[19]   "Journal of a Voyage", Yale ed., v. 1, pp. 78-79.
[20]   *Autobiography*, p. 114.

important Part" of his Journal,[21] has not been found, but the headings and the statement of purpose remain. Admitting that he had "never fixed a regular design in life", he determined that since he was entering a new scene of his life he would "henceforth . . . live in all respects like a rational creature". He resolved to be frugal until he had repaid his debts, to be truthful and sincere, to work diligently at his business without being diverted "by any foolish project of growing suddenly rich", and to "speak ill of no man whatever not even in a matter of truth".[22] In short, he seems to have desired "the name of an honest fellow".

This was his first known attempt at moral improvement and marks the beginning of the third stage in his changing religious attitudes. For the next ten years he moved away from skepticism and irresponsibility. He had begun to strive for moral improvement because it seemed rational and practical for him, but by 1734 he believed moral improvement important for all men and religious observances important for himself.

His ship reached Philadelphia in October 1726, and he worked for Denham until February 1726/27, when he became so ill that death seemed to him certain. Whether this close experience with death in any way influenced his future attitude is a matter of conjecture. Certainly his efforts toward self-improvement became more specific. In the autumn of 1727 he formed the Junto, with its dual purpose of self-improvement and the doing of public good. Probably in the fall of 1728 he and Hugh Meredith began their own printing business, and on November 20, 1728, Franklin composed his "Articles of Belief and Acts of Religion", the first certain indication that he had found rational morality alone unsatisfactory.

He conceived of God as a Being remote and incomprehensible to man, so "*Supremely Perfect*" that he is "INFINITELY ABOVE" desiring praise from "such an inconsiderable Nothing as Man". This "*Infinite Father*" had created gods greater than man, who "return him a more rational and glorious Praise". Each of these lesser gods had "made for himself, one glorious Sun, attended

21   *Ibid.*, p. 106.
22   "Plan of Conduct", Yale ed., v. 1, pp. 99-100.

with a beautiful and admirable System of Planets". Franklin, then, determined to pray to the Author of his particular system, who was wise and good, pleased with man's praise, offended when slighted, "and delight[ed] in the Happiness of those he [had] created".[23]

Within two years Franklin had not only set out to attain moral virtue through his own efforts and with the help of others, but had also supplied himself with a personal religious service.

Probably in 1732,[24] Franklin had written an essay for the Junto, titled "On the Providence of God in the Government of the World." God, he said, was a Being of wisdom, goodness, and power who "sometimes interferes by his particular Providence, and sets aside the Events which would otherwise have been produc'd in the Course of Nature, or by the Free Agency of Men".[25] He felt that the belief in Providence was "the Foundation of all true Religion",[26] and repeated this some 25 years later when he objected to "an Argument . . . against the Doctrine of a particular Providence. . . . For without the Belief of a Providence that takes Cognizance of, guards and guides and may favour particular Persons, there is no Motive to Worship a Deity, to fear its Displeasure, or to pray for its Protection." [27]

Sometime between 1728 and 1734, he was "prevail'd on" to attend church services "once for five Sundays successively", but, disappointed with the Rev. Jedediah Andrews' sermons, he returned to his own form of worship.[28] In 1734, however, a Presbyterian preacher named Samuel Hemphill came to assist Andrews, and Franklin found his sermons most satisfactory. Hemphill's emphasis upon good works made Franklin "one of his constant Hearers",[29] but also resulted in the Preacher's suspension by the Synod for "Heterodoxy".

Franklin defended Hemphill both before and after the sus-

23   "Articles of Belief and Acts of Religion", Yale ed., v. 1, pp. 102-103.
24   Ed's. note, Yale ed., v. 1, p. 264.
25   *Ibid.*, p. 268.
26   *Ibid.*, p. 269.
27   *Ibid.*, v. 7, p. 294.
28   *Autobiography*, pp. 147-148.
29   *Ibid.*, p. 167.

pension. Described by his detractors as "a *New-Light Man*, a *Deist*, one who preach'd nothing but *Morality*",[30] Hemphill upset those Philadelphia Presbyterians who had not adjusted faith and works as many Boston Congregationalists had done long before. Hemphill had not only preached that Christianity was God's second revelation – the first being the law of nature, but also "set up St. James against St. Paul".[31] He preached "that tho' it may be disputed how far ... Good Works ... are of themselves available for Salvation, yet it can't be denied but that they put Men in God's Way, reconcile him to 'em, and whatever else is wanting dispose him to reveal even that unto them".[32] To Hemphill, "Saving Faith ... is always attended with suitable Effects; that is, with Piety and Virtue, or Love to God and Mankind." [33]

Objecting strenuously to the methods of the Commission as much as to their dogmatic attitude, Franklin in his defense of Hemphill revealed a sustained anger and bitterness that cannot be found in any other of his writings. There is no doubt that he was very personally involved in the struggle. He defended Hemphill not only because he objected to injustice, but because he agreed with Hemphill that man's duty was to strive for moral virtue and *not* to rest content upon faith.

From the conclusion of the Hemphill affair until 1775, Franklin's religious beliefs remained fairly static. He worshipped God privately and gave financial support to many sects (among others, the Anglicans, Quakers, Jews, Presbyterians, and the "new light" preachers) although he rarely attended their services. As in 1734, he worked for his own moral improvement and believed firmly in encouraging others to do the same. Though he had already decided that religious observances were important to him, he now thought that religion might lead other men to virtue and happiness. In 1738 he wrote to his mother and father:

My Mother grieves that one of her Sons is an Arian, another an

---

30 "Observations on the Proceedings, 1735", Yale ed., v. 2, p. 39.
31 "Observations on the Proceedings against Mr. Hemphill", *ibid.*, p. 42.
32 "Observations on the Proceedings, 1735", *ibid.*, p. 61.
33 "Defense of the Observations, 1735", *ibid.*, p. 121.

Arminian. What an Arminian or an Arian is, I cannot say that I very well know; the Truth is, I make such Distinctions very little my Study; I think vital Religion has always suffer'd, when Orthodoxy is more regarded than Virtue. And the Scripture assures me, that at the last Day, we shall not be examin'd what we *thought*, but what we *did*; and our Recommendation will not be that we said *Lord, Lord*, but that we did GOOD to our Fellow Creatures.[34]

His statement concerning "vital Religion" best describes the beliefs he held for the greater part of his life.

Franklin spent the last fifteen years of his life working for the successful completion of the American Revolution. He took part in what he thought was "a miracle in human affairs". He had seen the colonies, suddenly deprived of any authorized government, form a new government and gather an army and navy, although they had "neither a ship of war, a company of soldiers, nor magazines, arms, artillery, or ammunition". Further, they had done all this "in the face of a most formidable invasion, by the most powerful nation, fully provided with armies, fleets, and all the instruments of destruction, powerfully allied and aided".[35] Franklin watched England's defeat by means he thought historically "rare" – "that in one War two Armies should be taken Prisoners completely, not a Man in either escaping"; or that an American expedition

so complex, form'd of Armies of different Nations, and of Land and Sea Forces, should with such perfect Concord be assembled from different Places by Land and Water, form their Junction punctually, without the least Retard by cross Accidents of Wind or Weather, or Interruption from the Enemy; and that the Army, which was their Object, should in the mean time have the Goodness to quit a Situation from whence it might have escaped, and place itself in another from whence an escape was impossible.[36]

He learned that the English Lord "who approved the burning of American houses, had had fire brought home to him",[37] and he

---

34 "To Josiah and Abiah Franklin", *ibid.*, p. 204.
35 Parton, v. 2, pp. 278-279.
36 "To John Adams", Smyth ed., v. 8, p. 333.
37 "To William Carmichael", *ibid.*, p. 99.

saw that even America's errors worked to her advantage. He concluded "*These are thy Doings, O Lord, and they are marvellous in our Eyes.*" [38]

After the ratification of the peace treaty, he wrote,

If I had ever before been an Atheist, I should now have been convinced of the Being and Government of a Deity! It is he who abases the Proud and favours the Humble. May we never forget his Goodness to us, and may our future Conduct manifest our Gratitude.[39]

Divine Providence had not only assisted America in attaining independence, but had designed that America should serve mankind in a special way. America's cause, he wrote in 1777, "is *the Cause of all Mankind*, ... 'Tis a glorious task assign'd us by Providence; which has, I trust, given us Spirit and Virtue equal to it, and will at last crown it with Success." [40] His faith in Providence was such that he could not believe an event as important as the framing of the American Constitution "should be suffered to pass without being in some degree influenc'd, guided, and governed by that omnipotent, omnipresent, and beneficent Ruler . . .".[41] As early as 1732 Franklin had expressed a belief in a particular Providence, but his wonder at what he thought God's intervention in America's behalf during the Revolution seems to indicate that his earlier statement may have represented an intellectual acceptance rather than a firm belief. Certainly by the end of the Revolution Franklin had added omnipresence to the attributes of his god.

In 1787, at the age of 81, Franklin acted as one of Pennsylvania's representatives at the Constitutional Convention. Concerned with the lack of agreement among the representatives, he moved that the delegates open their meetings with prayers for guidance. In the course of making his motion he explained quite clearly what had happened to his religious beliefs over the years:

I have lived, Sir, a long time; and the longer I live, the more con-

---

[38] "To Josiah Quincy", *ibid.*, v. 9, p. 94.
[39] "To William Strahan", *ibid.*, p. 262.
[40] "To Samuel Cooper", *ibid.*, v. 7, p. 56.
[41] "A Comparison of the Conduct of the Ancient Jews and of the Anti-Federalists in the United States of America", *ibid.*, v. 9, p. 703.

vincing proofs I see of this Truth, *that* GOD *governs in the Affairs of Men.* And if a Sparrow cannot fall to the Ground without his Notice, is it probable that an Empire can rise without his Aid? We have been assured, Sir, in the Sacred Writings, that 'except the Lord build the House, they labour in vain that build it' I firmly believe this; and I also believe, that, without his concurring Aid, we shall succeed in this political Building no better than the Builders of Babel. . . . [42]

Not only would their desires for unity be unfulfilled, he warned, but man's hope for future improvement might be destroyed, for ". . . Mankind may hereafter, from this unfortunate Instance, despair of establishing Government by human Wisdom, and leave it to Chance, War, and Conquest".[43] Benjamin Franklin at twenty would not have believed that prayers could influence the "Artificer" of a clock-like universe.[44] His notes record that " '*The Convention, except three or four Persons, thought Prayer unnecessary!!*' " [45]

Franklin's personal experiences seemed to continually strengthen his religious beliefs. Not only did his concept of Divine Providence come to resemble the theology of Boston Puritanism, but he seemed to be more and more aware of the irrational elements in man and his tendency toward evil. Again, it was the War that focused his attention on human evil. He wished that moral science could advance as he foresaw "*true* science" would, and that as men gained power over matter, so would they "cease to be Wolves to one another, and that human Beings would at length learn what they now improperly call Humanity!" [46] Sometimes his bitterness toward man's false pride and cruelty sounds remarkably like Mark Twain's.[47]

[42] "Motion for Prayers in the Convention", Smyth ed., v. 9, pp. 600-601.
[43] *Ibid.*
[44] "A Dissertation on Liberty and Necessity, Pleasure and Pain", Yale ed., v. 1, p. 62.
[45] Benjamin Franklin, "Motion", in P. L. Ford, *Many Sided Franklin* (New York, The Century Company, 1899), p. 169. Photograph of Franklin's comment showing the original punctuation.
[46] Smyth ed., v. 8, p. 10.
[47] In 1782, Franklin told an anecdote that bears an interesting resemblance to Mark Twain's unfinished story *The Mysterious Stranger* and also to the *Letters from the Earth.* Franklin wrote Priestley that "A young

Men I find to be a Sort of Beings very badly constructed, as they
are generally more easily provok'd than reconcil'd, more disposed to
do Mischief to each other than to make Reparation, much more
easily deceiv'd than undeceiv'd, and having more Pride and even
Pleasure in killing than in begetting one another; for without a
Blush they assemble in great armies at NoonDay to destroy, and when
they have kill'd as many as they can, they exaggerate the Number to
augment the fancied Glory; but they creep into Corners, or cover
themselves with the Darkness of night, when they mean to beget, as
being asham'd of a virtuous Action. A virtuous Action it would be,
and a vicious one the killing of them, if the Species were really worth
producing or preserving; but of this I begin to doubt.[48]

Though Franklin never stopped believing that man must strive
for himself and for those who would come after him, he was
very much aware that not all men would succeed. He combined
in his attitude toward man the optimism of the Enlightenment
and the realism of Puritanism. He thought that Hobbes' idea of
the state of nature was "somewhat nearer the Truth than that
which makes the State of Nature a State of Love; But the Truth
perhaps lies between both Extreams".[49]

Experience had taught Franklin that some men would lead
virtuous and happy lives while others would not – despite the
obvious advantages of virtue. Both he and Mather would have
agreed that a man's success depended upon God. As early as

Angel of Distinction being sent down to this world on some Business, for
the first time, had an old courier-spirit assigned him as a Guide. They
arriv'd over the Seas of Martinico, in the middle of the long Day of
obstinate Fight between the Fleets of Rodney and De Grasse. When thro'
the Clouds of smoke, he saw the Fire of the Guns, the Decks covered with
mangled Limbs, and Bodies dead or dying; the ships sinking, burning, or
blown into the Air; and the Quantity of Pain, Misery, and Destruction, the
Crews yet alive were thus with so much Eagerness dealing round to one
another; he turn'd angrily to his Guide, and said, 'You blundering Block-
head, you are ignorant of your Business; you undertook to conduct me to
the Earth, and you have brought me into Hell!' 'No, Sir', says the Guide,
'I have made no mistake; this is really the Earth, and these are men. Devils
never treat one another in this cruel manner; they have more Sense, and
more of what Men (vainly) call *Humanity*' " ("To J. Priestley", Smyth
ed., v. 8, pp. 452-453).
[48]   "To Joseph Priestley", Smyth ed., v. 8, pp. 451-452.
[49]   "To James Logan", Yale ed., v. 2, p. 185.

1732, Franklin had considered that a rational creature's happiness lay first in "a Sound Mind" which is "A Faculty of reasoning justly and truly in searching after [and] discovering such truths as relate to my Happiness." And this faculty was "the Gift of God, capable of being improv'd by Experience and Instruction, into Wisdom".[50] He was certain that "none but God can at the same time give good Counsel, and Wisdom to make use of it".[51]

Franklin realistically accepted man as potentially good or evil, and he accepted death with an equally matter-of-fact attitude. "All that ever were born are either dead, or must die. It becomes us to submit, and to comfort ourselves with the hope of a better life and more happy meeting hereafter." [52] The things of this world, he wrote, "are changeable, uncertain, transitory . . .; but his Favour, if we can secure it, is an Inheritance for ever".[53] Though death was real, it was not frightening. Mather had felt that to fear death was to "*dishonor*" his Saviour,[54] and Franklin, too, would "chearfully, with filial Confidence", resign his spirit.[55]

Franklin was as scrupulous in examining his motives as were those Puritans who believed that "guilt or innocence consisted not in what was done but in what was intended".[56] Franklin had considered among the Junto "Queries", "Whether Men ought to be denominated Good or ill Men from their Actions or their Inclinations." [57] In 1756 he had apparently been concerned with his motives in opposing the Proprietors of Pennsylvania but finally concluded that he acted "from a Regard to the Publick Good. I may be mistaken in what is that Publick Good; but at least I mean well." [58] A man was to be judged good, he thought, by "his disposition to do good", as well as by "his constant endeavours and

---

50   "Queries to be ask'd the Junto", *ibid.*, v. 1, p. 262.
51   "To James Hutton", Smyth ed., v. 7, p. 99.
52   "To Mrs. Catherine Greene", *ibid.*, v. 4, p. 216.
53   "To Mrs. Deborah Franklin", Smyth ed., v. 4, pp. 383-384.
54   Samuel Mather, *The Life of the Very Reverend and Learned Cotton Mather* (Boston, 1729), p. 149.
55   "To Jonathan Shipley", Smyth ed., v. 9, p. 491.
56   Perry Miller, *The New England Mind: The Seventeenth Century* (Cambridge, Harvard University Press, 1954), p. 52.
57   Yale ed., v. 1, p. 263. Ed's. footnote, "Struck out in the draft".
58   "To Peter Collinson", *ibid.*, v. 7, p. 14.

success in doing it".[59] And even the "ancient" ephemera of the well known bagatelle enjoyed as one of his few remaining solid pleasures "the reflection of a long life spent in meaning well".[60]

Though Franklin did not believe that he would merit Heaven by performing good works,[61] he does not seem to have doubted his own state of grace. He thought that God had looked after him in this life, had blessed him with good things, and had made even his chastisements ultimately beneficial. Therefore he did not doubt that God loved him and would continue to care for him "not only here but hereafter".[62]

However Franklin's religion may be labeled, there was very little in it after 1726 that Mather would have objected to. Like Franklin, Mather worshipped God privately and thought the "*Religion of the Closett*" conformed closely to Christ's worship of God.[63] Although the "ability of praying rightly [was] a peculiar gift",[64] the form of personal prayers was not prescribed. Mather advised the candidates for the ministry that he could not "commend any *Liturgy* . . . . I can do no other than tell you. . . . That *in old times*, there *was no Form of Prayer prescribed* for all to be bound unto, but every One might *make what Prayer* he *pleased,* if but the *Analogy of Faith* were kept unto." [65] If God were to be glorified, however, His Perfections must be beheld with a "suitable *Veneration*".[66] The first part of Franklin's religion of the closet was Adoration, a preliminary stage designed to produce the necessary veneration. He felt that his "Soul ought to be calm and Serene", that his Countenance should express "a filial

---

59 "To John Coakley Lettsom", Smyth ed., v. 9, p. 16.
60 "The Ephemera", *ibid.*, v. 7, p. 209.
61 "To Joseph Huey", Yale ed., v. 4, p. 505.
62 "To George Whitfield", Smyth ed., v. 4, p. 248.
63 *Diary of Cotton Mather*, ed. by Worthington Chauncey Ford (= *Massachusetts Historical Society Collections*, Seventh Series) (Boston, Published by the Society, 1911), v. 8, p. 560. Hereafter v. 8 designated *Diary*, 2 and v. 7, designated *Diary*, 1.
64 John Calvin, *Institutes of the Christian Religion*, tr. and collated John Allen, 7th American edition, revised and corrected (Philadelphia, Presbyterian Board of Christian Education, n.d.), III, 20.5.
65 *Manuductio*, pp. 111-112.
66 *Ibid.*, p. 8.

Respect, mixt with a kind of Smiling, that signifies inward Joy, and Satisfaction, and Admiration".[67] Then he could proceed to praise the Creator for the wonder, power, wisdom, and goodness of his creation.

His prayers reflected the general attitudes of New England Puritanism. Like Mather, he believed that one should "Pray as if [he] were to die tomorrow." [68] Calvin had written, "we must pray for no more than God permits",[69] and Franklin's "Petition" recognized that "We cannot be Certain that many Things Which we often hear mentioned in the Petitions of Men to the Deity, would prove REAL GOODS if they were in our Possession", and so left to God the granting of "such Things".[70] He drew upon his New England background when he suggested Pennsylvania's first General Fast to give thanks to God and "humbly pray for his Protection".[71]

Neither Calvin [72] nor Mather would have disagreed with Franklin's concept of God as a Being who "is pleased and delights in the Happiness of those he has created; ... And since he has created many Things which seem purely design'd for the Delight of Man, I believe he is not offended when he sees his Children solace themselves in any manner of pleasant Exercises and innocent Delights." [73] Mather saw "every creature . . . enstamped with

[67] "Articles of Belief and Acts of Religion", Yale ed., v. 1, p. 104.
[68] "Poor Richard", 1757, *ibid.*, v. 7, p. 81.
[69] John Calvin, Bk. III, 20.5.
[70] "Articles of Belief and Acts of Religion", Yale ed., v. 1, p. 107.
[71] *Ibid.*, v. 3, pp. 228-229.
[72] "It must be laid down as a principle, that the use of the gifts of God is not erroneous when it is directed to the same end for which the Creator himself has created and appointed them for us; since he has created them for our benefit, not for our injury. Wherefore, no one will observe a more proper rule, than he who shall diligently regard this end. Now, if we consider for what end he has created the various kinds of aliment, we shall find that he intended to provide not only for our necessity, but likewise for our pleasure and delight. ... But shall the Lord have endued flowers with such beauty, to present itself to our eyes, with such sweetness of smell, to impress our sense of smelling; and shall it be unlawful for our eyes to be affected with the beautiful sight, or our olfactory nerves with the agreeable odour? What! has he not made such a distinction of colours as to render some more agreeable than others?" (John Calvin, Bk. III, 10.2).
[73] "Articles of Belief and Acts of Religion", Yale ed., v. 1, p. 103.

characters of the divine goodness".[74] The works of God, the
creatures and the earth itself, were wonderful. "Our good God
has ordered it, that whatever is natural is delightful, and has a
tendency to good. . . . Great God, thou art good, and thou dost
good; O teach me thy statutes!" [75] Like Franklin he saw

all Creatures every where full of their *Delights.* . . . 'Tis a marvellous
Display of infinite Goodness. The Good God has made His Creatures
capable of *Delights*; He accommodates them with continual *Delights.*
Their Delights are the delicious Entertainments of His infinite *Good-
ness.* His *Goodness* takes Pleasure, and is delighted, in the Delights of
His Creatures.[76]

Because both men believed that God enjoyed the delights of his
creatures and because they believed that God was to be thanked,
they took periodic inventories of their blessings. In the *Essays to
Do Good* Mather had suggested that one should make "a List of
the more distinguishable Succours, and Bounties, wherewith our
God has comforted us".[77] Mather had praised and thanked God
for his charming, obliging, efficient, and honorable wife, for the
fifteen years they had shared together, and for his "lovely Off-
Spring".[78] Periodically he thanked God for his library and facili-
ties for study.[79] Franklin regularly thanked God in his prayers for
all the good things of the earth and periodically reviewed, as
Mather had, the things with which he had been blessed. Each re-
writing of his will listed his blessings and formally gave thanks to
God:

And now humbly returning sincere Thanks to GOD for producing me
into Being, and conducting me hitherto thro' Life so happily, so free
from Sickness, Pain and Trouble, and with such a Competency of
this World's Goods as might make a reasonable Mind easy: That he
was pleased to give me such a Mind, with moderate Passions, or so
much of his gracious Assistance in governing them; and to free it
early from Ambition, Avarice and Superstition, . . . That he gave me

[74] *The Christian Philosopher* (Charlestown, Published at the Middlesex
Bookstore, 1815), p. 149. Microfilm.
[75] *Ibid.*, p. 233.
[76] *Diary*, 1, p. 553.
[77] *Essays to Do Good*, p. 47.
[78] *Diary*, 1, p. 405.
[79] *Ibid.*, p. 36.

to live so long in a Land of Liberty, with a People that I love, and rais'd me, tho' a Stranger, so many Friends among them; bestowing on me moreover a loving and prudent Wife, and dutiful Children.[80]

Like many other men of the eighteenth century, they expressed views generally associated with Deism. Though some critics have thought of Franklin's Deism in the more recent sense of the word – which emphasizes the positive nature of "theism" and the negative nature of "deism" (*OED*) – Franklin himself equated a "deist" with a "theist" and opposed his "theist" or "deist" to an "atheist".[81] His early pamphlet denying man's moral responsibility and spiritual immortality [82] represented only a brief period in his religious development. He not only cited this pamphlet as one of his "errata" but tried to destroy the existing copies lest they have a bad influence. He never again seriously attacked the foundations of religious beliefs, and he discouraged others from doing so.

Though Mather referred to "deism" as "Atheistical Theism",[83] he searched, as had Lord Herbert of Cherbury, for that which God "has ordained unchangeable",[84] for that which rational man could discern as true. To Mather it was "unnatural" to be "irreligious".[85] Even a Mohammedan, he wrote, "without any teacher, but reason" was "led on to the acknowledgment of a glorious God", for Nature, too, might teach.[86] Like many Deists he thought of the universe as a "mighty engine, of an extent that cannot be measured",[87] operating under fixed laws which "continue this day according to [God's] ordinances".[88]

But most of all, Mather looked for "the Maxims of the ever-

---

[80]   "Last Will and Testament", Yale ed., v. 3, pp. 481-482.
[81]   "To Cadwallader Colden", Smyth ed., v. 2, p. 322.
[82]   "A Dissertation on Liberty and Necessity, Pleasure and Pain", Yale ed., v. 1, pp. 58-71.
[83]   *The Diary of Cotton Mather D.D., F.R.S. for the Year 1712*, ed. by William R. Manierre (Charlottesville, Va., The University Press of Virginia, 1964), II, p. 61.
[84]   *De Religione Laici*, ed. by Harold Hutcheson (New Haven, Yale University Press, 1944), p. 113.
[85]   *Essays to Do Good*, p. 126.
[86]   *The Christian Philosopher*, pp. 9-10.
[87]   *Ibid.*, p. 174.
[88]   *Ibid.*, p. 38.

lasting Gospel; the glorious Maxims wherein all the Children of God really are united".[89] Bemoaning "the Antichristian Spirit of *Sectarism*", he tried to "Contract into a little Room, *the Sum of the Matter*, and the PIETY, which will be found a *Sure Foundation* for an UNION among all Parties of True CHRISTIANS, however they may be Denominated or Distinguished".[90] He put forth three major beliefs: first, the concept of God whom man must "*Serve* and *Please*"; second, the belief in Christ, the Redeemer, who will "*judge the World*"; and third, "Out of Respect unto GOD and His CHRIST, I must heartily *Love my Neighbour*, and forever do unto *Other Men*, as I must own it Reasonable for them to do unto *myself*." [91]

Considering that the world needed people who desired the "good of mankind" rather than party or private interests, Franklin made up "the Substance of an intended Creed" which he felt was "free of every thing that might shock the Professors of any Religion". This creed maintained:

> That there is one God who made all things.
> That he governs the World by his Providence.
> That he ought to be worshipped by Adoration,
>   Prayer and Thanksgiving.
> But that the most acceptable Service of God
>   is doing Good to Man.
> That the Soul is immortal.
> And that God will certainly reward Virtue and
>   punish Vice either here or hereafter.[92]

Both Mather and Franklin shared a belief in a God to whom man owed tribute. Both acknowledged that there would be a final judgment and emphasized doing good to other men as a service or tribute to God. Although they were not in absolute agreement on the elements they considered essential, at least they believed in the possibility and importance of a single creed. Their purpose, again, reflects their desire to do good. Sectarian variations lead to

[89] *Diary*, 2, p. 329.
[90] *Manuductio*, p. 117.
[91] *Ibid.*, p. 118.
[92] *Autobiography*, p. 162.

dissension and may deter man from his most important duty to God – his obligation to man – not to help save a man's soul at the expense of his life, as the inquisitors had done, but to help man live fully in this life and still enjoy heaven.

The quite obvious difference between their creeds seems to be Franklin's omission of "Christ, the Redeemer". In a letter to Ezra Stiles, written little more than a month before his death, Franklin said,

As to Jesus of Nazareth, my Opinion of whom you particularly desire, I think the System of Morals and his Religion, as he left them to us, the best the World ever saw or is likely to see; but I apprehend it has received various corrupting Changes, and I have, with most of the present Dissenters in England, some Doubts as to his Divinity.[93]

Although Franklin omitted Christ from his public creed and questioned His Divinity, he seems to have found it necessary to include in his personal creed a being who functioned as a mediator between man and God. Drawing up his "Articles of Belief" Franklin acknowledged the infinite superiority of God and the overwhelming inferiority of man and concluded that the God responsible for creating the Newtonian universe could not be content with man's puny prayers. But because man had a natural desire to worship "SOMETHING",[94] it was not inconceivable that there were lesser gods, the "Sons of Light" created by the Father of Lights to make and rule over their own systems of planets.[95] Franklin's mediating god seems to have reconciled the incomprehensibility of God and the vastness of His creation with a belief in Providence; he seems also to represent a fulfillment of

---

[93] Smyth ed., v. 10, p. 84.

[94] "Articles of Belief and Acts of Religion", Yale ed., v. 1, p. 102.

[95] Franklin used Milton's phrase "Sons of Light" in his personal worship, and, in 1787 at the Constitutional Convention, moved that the members apply "to the Father of Lights to illuminate our Understandings" ("Motion for Prayers in the Convention", Smyth ed., v. 9, p. 600). Cotton Mather, in *The Christian Philosopher* had referred to God several times as the "father of lights" (p. 36) both in the sense of physical light and the light of reason. Franklin was probably familiar with Mather's book by 1787 for it is listed in the 1764 catalogue of Franklin's Library Company (I. W. Riley, *American Philosophy*, pp. 242-243).

man's desire to approach God without offending and with the hope of being heard.

William C. Bruce thought Franklin's creed "as eccentric as the Oriental notion that the whole world is upheld by a cow with blue horns".[96] Actually Franklin's concept was not as peculiar in his day as it seemed to Bruce. Students of astronomy by the end of the seventeenth century could conceive of a universe in which an unknown and possibly infinite number of planets circled majestically about their particular suns, bound in set groups by the force of gravity. Apparently influenced by this concept, Sir Isaac Newton, in a conversation with Mr. Conduitt on the night of March 7, 1724/25, had "seemed to doubt whether there were not intelligent beings superior to us who superintended these revolutions of the heavenly bodies by the direction of the Supreme Being".[97] Franklin may have heard of Newton's idea from Dr. Pemberton (for in 1725 Franklin was in London and knew Dr. Pemberton), or he may have been familiar with such a concept as it appeared in Plato's *Timaeus* or in the writings of John Locke, Sir Thomas Browne, Joseph Addison, Edward Young,[98] or the scientific speculators.

Cotton Mather, impressed by Newtonian astronomy, had drawn from some of these physico-theologians [99] the idea that God might have created beings lesser than He but greater than man. Drawing

[96]   Bruce, p. 77.

[97]   "A Remarkable and Curious Conversation Between Sir Isaac Newton and Mr. Conduitt", Appendix No. III, *The Life of Sir Isaac Newton*, by Sir David Brewster (London, William Tegg and Co., 1875), pp. 323-325.

[98]   *See* John Locke, "An Essay Concerning Human Understanding", *The Works of John Locke* (London, Printed for John Churchill and Sam Manship, 1714), v. 1, III, 6, 12, pp. 203-204; Sir Thomas Browne, *Religio Medici* (London, J. M. Dent & Sons, reprint 1931), pp. 37-40; Edward Young, *Night Thoughts* (New York, A. S. Barnes & Co., 1853), Book VI; Joseph Addison, *The Spectator*, No's. 408, 519, 621.

[99]   Kenneth Murdock believes that Mather's book *The Christian Philosopher* was drawn generally from Nehemiah Grew's *Cosmologia Sacra*, George Cheyne's *Philosophical Principles of Natural Religion*, William Derham's *Physico-Theology, or a Demonstration of the Being and Attributes of God from His Works of Creation*, and John Ray's *Wisdom of God Manifested in the Works of the Creation*, and *Physico-Theological Discourses* ("Introduction", *Cotton Mather Selections*, New York, Hafner Publishing Co., 1926, reprint, n.d., pp. xlix-l).

from Dr. Grew's theories, Mather considered that God might have created a series of beings with faculties superior to man's – some lesser beings who were embodied intellects, and higher beings who were all mind. And he did not find such a theory inimical to a belief in Christ, for "The highest perfection that any created mind can arise to, is that in the soul of our admirable Saviour, which is indeed embodied; but it is the soul of the Man who is personally united to the Son of God." [100] Contemplating the vastness of space, Mather wondered at the "dimensions" of the stars and the kinds of creatures God had chosen to replenish those worlds. "Who can tell what angelic inhabitants may there see and sing the praises of the Lord!" [101] For "If God has made such a multitude of stars, who can doubt, that he has by far a greater number of heavenly spirits, who are continually singing his praise." [102]

The vastness of the Newtonian universe opened the door for speculation about the existence of lesser gods, created by God to render Him praise and help in the operation of the universe. But this was not a new idea. When Mather referred to such beings he sometimes considered them in Platonic terms – pure mind or disembodied intellects; at other times he referred to them as angels. Ernest Benz, considering Mather's relationship to the pietist August Francke, noticed that Mather seemed to consider angels especially important as mediators or servants carrying out the activities of the Holy Ghost.[103] This concept not only tends to move God somewhat farther away from the creation (as many Deists believed God was) but also fits very well with the belief in a Chain of Being. Both Mather and Franklin had recognized a "scale of nature" which Mather measured from a stone to a man, and from man, "the equator of the universe", to "several orders of embodied intellect before we come to pure mind",[104] and which

[100] *The Christian Philosopher*, pp. 310-311.
[101] *Ibid.*, p. 24.
[102] *Ibid.*, p. 23.
[103] "Pietist and Puritan Sources of Early Protestant World Missions", *Church History*, 20 : 46, 1951.
[104] *The Christian Philosopher*, pp. 310-311.

Franklin measured from the oyster to the elephant, from the elephant to man, and from man to God.[105]

But Newtonian astronomy had only confirmed what Puritan theology had long known, that God was infinitely great, powerful and inscrutable, while man was finite and weak – a poor creature to offer praise to such a mighty Being. To Mather there was no doubt that if each fixed star were a sun with a system of its own, "How is it possible to consider the grandeur of our God, without annihilating ourselves before him?" [106] He quoted from Sir Francis Bacon's statement "that God is so holy, as that it is impossible for him to be pleased in any creature, though the work of his own hands, without beholding the same in the face of a Mediator; . . . that so in the person of the Mediator the true ladder might be fixed, whereby God might descend to his creatures, and his creatures ascend to him".[107]

Franklin's peculiar "cow with blue horns" must be understood, then, not only in terms of its function in allowing man to approach God, or its possible similarity to Platonic thought, or its correspondence with the Chain of Being concept, but also in terms of Newtonian science. While Mather indiscriminately used Platonic theory, astronomy, or Christian angels to refer to those beings greater than man, Franklin seems to have used only scientific concepts. He believed that each sun represented the existence of a god and that these gods might not be immortal, for "it may be that after many Ages, they are changed, and Others supply their Places".[108] His concern with the possibility of mortality for the lesser gods seems to reflect the belief of astronomers that the sun's regular loss of strength indicated that it had been created and therefore would not have eternal existence.[109] Franklin's god, like the sun, was a creation and so was not assured of eternal life.

Though Franklin felt that the figure of a mediating god was both appropriate and necessary, he did not acknowledge Christ as divine. Mather, however, except for very rare moments of

[105] "An Arabian Tale", Smyth ed., v. 10, p. 124.
[106] *The Christian Philosopher*, p. 37.
[107] *Ibid.*, p. 318.
[108] "Articles of Belief and Acts of Religion", Yale ed., v. 1, p. 103.
[109] *The Christian Philosopher*, pp. 35-36.

doubt, believed in Christ's divinity. And the two men also differed on the value of Revelation. Mather's faith in Revelation
was such that his son reports he would pick up with "respect"
from the streets any papers that had fallen from Bibles, regarding
them as possible sources of special guidance.[110] Franklin had not
so particularly revered the Bible. But Mather's position toward
Revelation seems to have changed during his lifetime. In 1715,
he began to try to dig "from the Mines of the Sacred Scriptures"
those maxims that were "everlasting", that would really unite the
"Children of God", and was willing to have the "lesser points . . .
depressed into their due subordination", so that men might dispute only these lesser points without bloodshed or sacrilege.[111]
This seems to imply that he was willing to consider some parts of
the Scriptures as more sacred than other parts.

It is probably not unusual that Benjamin Franklin's religious
beliefs went almost full circle from the theology of his childhood
to Deism and back again to the general beliefs of Boston Puritanism. He believed in a remote, incomprehensible God; prayed and
gave thanks to a mediating god; and believed that though many
men might be evil, some men, through their own efforts and with
God's help, could be good. But Franklin never lost the spirit of
Deism either, for he recognized that his belief was one of many
and that all men might worship in their own way without violating
the spirit of "vital religion". There has been no adequate study
of Mather's intellectual or religious development. But it is interesting to speculate how far he would have gone to encourage the
philosophical, i.e. scientific, and evangelical religion he tried so
hard to discern from the Scriptures so that "*all men should hearken
to Reason: And, . . . a World of Evil . . . be prevented in the
World, if men would once become so Reasonable*".[112] Both men
had been, at the same time, followers of Practical Piety and
reasonable religion.

---

[110] Samuel Mather, p. 23.
[111] *Diary*, 2, p. 329.
[112] *Ibid*., p. 542.

IV

SHOW THYSELF A MAN

Time and circumstances seem to have conspired in forming Cotton Mather's image as a witch-burning villain who was never part of the mainstream of American thought. Actually, Mather's role in the development of American culture was an important one, for he served as a bridge between seventeenth century supernaturalism and the Enlightenment. He prepared the way for Franklin and even for Jonathan Edwards, who was to carry on the theological innovations of *The Christian Philosopher* into a thorough reworking of the Puritan frame of reference. The popular concept of Cotton Mather needs revision, for he was not really a villain and his beliefs were as much a part of the American tradition as were Benjamin Franklin's. In fact, understanding the relationship of Mather to Franklin is essential for a comprehension of the development of our cultural pattern.

In his own way, Benjamin Franklin also needs to be rescued. He has been so often characterized in terms of *Poor Richard's Almanac* that his image has become a caricature. To consider him only as a man after the main chance is to forget that he spent the better part of his adult life working in the interest of others. To consider that he valued only utility is to forget that he began his electrical studies with no hope of practical results. But perhaps the greatest misunderstanding of his character has been a general assumption that he was irreligious, lacked any spiritual qualities, or at best, valued morality only because it was useful. Though he used the argument of utility to influence others, he was far too intelligent and had much too keen a sense of humor to be taken in by his own bait. Though he followed no specific orthodoxy, he was not, as many critics have maintained, devoid of religious feeling.

Certainly both Franklin and Mather were alike in the causes they favored – religious toleration, education, and science; and underlying their activities was a similar faith in the possibility of human achievement. In this, both showed themselves to be solidly in the American tradition. Like others whom Ralph Barton Perry considered characteristically American, Mather and Franklin refused to "regard unhappiness as the necessary lot of man".[1] They hoped for "perpetual and limitless improvement",[2] and they acknowledged "the force of evil and ... the inertia and indifference of inanimate nature, coupled with an ideal of the good and a belief in man's power to achieve it by the contrived and combined efforts of individuals".[3] Like other Americans, their faith was founded upon

no worship of the past, no assurance that all is perfect in the eternal constitution of things, or in another world, but [it was] ... a conditional faith: *we can if we try*, and put our minds and our hands to it, and unite our action.[4]

The American's traditionally optimistic belief in man's ability to solve his problems has persisted in American culture from Cotton Mather's time to the present. After Franklin's death in 1792, the general spirit of optimism continued to grow as American nationalism grew. But important changes in the structure of American culture at the end of the nineteenth century upset, for a while, the optimism prevailing among intellectuals. The work of Darwin, Frazer, Freud, and Marx reduced modern man from his traditional position as the apex of God's creation to a limited creature irrevocably related to the animal kingdom and trapped between internal libidinal forces and external cultural pressures. American psychology, by adopting Pavlov's theories of conditioned responses and Freud's theories of the distribution of psychic energy as explanations for the nature of man, helped reinforce

[1] *Characteristically American* (New York, Alfred A. Knopf, 1949), p. 12.
[2] *Ibid.*, p. 16.
[3] *Ibid.*, pp. 26-27.
[4] *Ibid.*, pp. 32-33.

man's sense of helplessness and his feeling that existence was devoid of meaning.

But the traditional American belief in an active, striving man has in recent years found new expression in the writings of men who sometimes describe themselves as existential psychologists or as representatives of a "Third Force" in American psychology. They count among their adherents Adlerians, Rankians, Jungians, neo-Freudians, post-Freudians, followers of Kurt Goldstein's organismic-psychology, Gestalt and Lewinian psychologists, general semanticists, personality psychologists, Self-psychologists, and growth-psychologists, as well as those associated specifically with existential psychology and psychiatry.[5] While the members of this Third Force agree upon no fully elaborated theory, they do agree that the Pavlovian or stimulus-response theories and the various Freudian theories provide an inadequate explanation for the nature of man. In general they recognize the importance of the stimulus-response theories, but point out that these deal only with man's peripheral motives and actions. They maintain that Freudian theory provides only a "psychopathology of the average"[6] because it defines mental illness in terms of the degree of deviation from standard behavior. Underlying their general rejection of a totally mechanistic explanation for man's behavior is a refusal to accept man as a creature who desires only to be at rest, who exists only to wish for an escape from tensions and anxieties, who seeks eternally for a static position of non-wanting.

In place of a passive man, the Third Force writers posit man as an active growing organism. Utilizing data from the Pavlovian and Freudian schools, they go on to consider man from what Gordon Allport calls the Leibnitzian position – one that conceives of man as not only acted upon but acting from within.[7] They assume that man reaches physical maturity through a developmental process and achieves mental maturity through a similar process – an unfolding of his individual and generic nature. All-

[5]   Abraham H. Maslow, "Preface", *Toward a Psychology of Being* (Princeton, New Jersey, D. Van Nostrand Company, Inc., 1962), p. vi.

[6]   *Ibid.*, p. 15.

[7]   Gordon W. Allport, *Becoming* (New Haven, Yale University Press, 1962), p. 12.

port describes this growth process of "becoming" as one governed
by "a disposition to realize . . . possibilities, i.e., to become characteristically human at all stages of development".[8] Abraham
Maslow refers to a similar process by the term "self-actualization",
which he believes "stresses 'full-humanness', the development of
the biologically based nature of man, [which] therefore is (em-
pirically) normative for the whole species rather than for particular times and places".[9]

It is in the concept of the self-actualized individual that the
basic beliefs of Cotton Mather and Benjamin Franklin seem to be
restated – not only in the obvious emphasis upon the possibility
for human "becoming", but also because of a certain similarity
of method and a recognition that such an end is not easily
achieved.

Although Mather's and Franklin's Practical Piety tended to
stress the possibility of man's accomplishment, their optimism
was always based upon an implicit acceptance of what has sometimes been called the grimmer aspects of Calvinism. Perry Miller
believes that the real being of Puritanism "was not in its doctrines
but behind them; the impetus came from an urgent sense of
man's predicament, from a mood so deep that it could never be
completely articulated".[10] Practical Piety was founded upon this
sense of man's predicament, but it tended to stress the belief that
man, making the most of limited assets, would somehow "over-
come". It is in this sense that we may best understand why Puritanism remained such a potent force in American thought.

Like other Puritans, Mather and Franklin accepted the existence of a remote and incomprehensible God, who had created a
splendid universe operating under fixed laws. Here, far from God,
man lived, restricted by his ignorance of eternal secrets, sentenced
to experience pain and death as well as pleasure, and condemned,
because of his reason, to a full awareness of his position. Each
man contained within himself the potential for good or evil, and

---

8   *Ibid.*, p. 27.
9   Maslow, p. iii.
10   *The New England Mind: The Seventeenth Century* (Cambridge, Harvard University Press, 1954), p. 4.

though good would seem to be the goal for which all men must logically strive, not all men would even try. Only he who had God's help or grace could do good – that is, develop himself intellectually and morally so that he could fulfill the purpose of his existence, doing good for others. However, to develop himself fully as a man, the individual did not wait for grace – he Prepared himself by accepting, intellectually, certain realities: first, the inevitability of death; second, the limited nature of his ability as a man; and third, the necessity for enjoying rationally the satisfaction of his physical needs. He examined, as best he could, his desires, his talents, and the means available to him for utilizing them. Armed with an increased understanding of his own nature and abilities, he proceeded to act in accordance with what he thought was his final purpose – fulfilling his duty to God, which was best accomplished by doing good to God's creation, man. And he accepted responsibility for his actions.

Comparison of the process of Preparation for Justification with the preliminary motions necessary for self-actualization reveals striking similarities. Underlying the possibility for achieving human maturity is the necessity for an awareness of "all the discordant conditions of our own existence" [11] – that is, the existence of death, disease, and pain as well as life, health, and pleasure. The natural world, being neutral, will accommodate man only if man will accommodate himself to it. In this world man is limited by his ignorance, which will never be fully removed, as well as by genetic inheritance and chance environmental factors. Not only have the Third Force writers recognized man's so-called higher and lower natures, but Abraham Maslow has postulated a hierarchy of human motivation in which higher needs are not felt until the more elementary needs are fulfilled. Physiological needs must be satisfied first; needs related to safety (including consistency and security) are second; love (including affection and a sense of belonging as well as sexual love) is third; esteem ("based upon real capacity, achievement and respect") is fourth; and then, only after these "pre-potent" needs have re-

[11]   Allport, p. 79.

ceived at least minimal satisfaction, can the need for self-actualization be felt.[12]

To reach the state where self-actualization is possible, man must satisfy those needs he shares with other animals. He becomes something more than an animal not when he tries to deny the fire in his belly but when, by appeasement, he frees himself from the flames. Franklin's attitude toward money can best be understood in similar terms. The possession of a sufficient amount of money in a mercantile society provides the simplest means for attaining release from the grosser human needs.[13] Therefore, thrift is important because it may enable some men to achieve an existence more meaningful than one devoted only to gaining a subsistence. Mather, Franklin, and the Third Force writers would have agreed that it is very "hard for an empty Bag to stand upright".

After a man's elementary needs have been satisfied directly, or indirectly through sublimation, he must proceed to study himself. We must look within ourselves, Maslow writes, to try to determine the

unconscious and preconscious perception of our own nature, of our own destiny, or our own capacities, of our own 'call' in life. [The internal conscience] insists that we be true to our inner nature and that we do not deny it out of weakness or for any other reason. He who belies his talent, the born painter who sells stockings instead, the intelligent man who lives a stupid life, . . . all these people perceive in a deep way that they have done wrong to themselves and despise themselves for it. Out of this self-punishment may come only neurosis, but there may equally well come renewed courage, righteous indigna-

---

[12] "A Theory of Human Motivation", *Psychological Review*, 50 : 370-396, 1943. Maslow does not attempt to define the degree of fulfillment necessary for the emergence of the next potent need. Not only do individual variations make such a task seem impossible, but there is also the difficulty of distinguishing the dominating need, for "no need or drive can be treated as if it were isolated or discrete" (p. 370).

[13] This position contrasts with that found in Luke 6 : 20, "Blessed be ye poor; for yours is the kingdom of God." One might note, however, as R. H. Tawney does, that Calvinism, "as a way of life and a theory of society, . . . possessed from the beginning one characteristic which was both novel and important. It assumed an economic organization which was relatively advanced, and expounded its social ethics on the basis of it" (*Religion and the Rise of Capitalism*, New York, Harcourt, Brace and Company, c1926, p. 102).

tion, increased self-respect because of thereafter doing the right thing; in a word, growth and improvement can come through pain and conflict.[14]

For Maslow, the punishment for the denial of one's talents or "call" might be neurosis. For Franklin and Mather it might be physical or mental discomfort in this life as well as eternal punishment. But for all three the failure to fulfill oneself is the evil that demands atonement.

Once some degree of self-understanding is reached, the Third Force writers expect man "to accept and participate in the historical, temporal, spatial, biological, psychological, sociological conditions of [life] with such clarity of vision and acceptance of responsibility, and such courage as [he] can muster".[15] Though they recognize that "there are upper limits to the possibilities of growth in each life", they believe it is likely "that these limits are movable by virtue of the capacities for reflection, for self-objectification, and to a degree by breadth of education, and by the effort an individual may put forth".[16] Cotton Mather, Benjamin Franklin, and Gordon Allport would have agreed that man must make the most of his intellectual capacities, act thoughtfully, and accept responsibility for his actions.

Before self-actualization is possible, man must recognize the conditions of his existence, accept his isolation, and be aware of "the dimension of seriousness and profundity of living (or perhaps the 'tragic sense of life') contrasted with the shallow and superficial life, which is a kind of diminished living, a defense against the ultimate problems of life".[17] At the same time he must be very aware of possibilities, of future time or becoming. Neither Mather nor Franklin was unaware of life's seriousness or of the effects which present actions might have upon the future – their own or mankind's.

Not only does the preparation for self-actualization resemble Preparation for Justification, but the characteristics of the self-

---

14   *Toward a Psychology of Being*, p. 6.
15   Allport, p. 79.
16   *Ibid.*, p. 88.
17   Maslow, *Toward a Psychology of Being*, p. 13.

actualized man are very much like those attributed to the Sanctified of Practical Piety. The individual who has achieved self-actualization "by virtue of what he has become, assumes a new relation to his society and indeed, to society in general. He not only transcends himself in various ways; he also transcends his culture." [18] Franklin and Mather thought of themselves both as Americans and as part of what they hoped would be a union of all men. The self-actualized man also believes, as Franklin and Mather did, in a kind of restricted optimism. Whether God or chance is the determining force, some men will be "saved" and come close to achieving their potential as human beings, whereas others will be "damned" to only partial growth. But a knowledge of the difficulties involved in helping all men achieve fulfillment will not keep the self-actualized man from trying. The Third Force writers believe implicitly that the fully matured man will work for the good of others.

Although God plays no specific part in the writings of most Third Force psychologists, they do leave room for Him in their speculations. Harold Grier McCurdy, a psychologist whose sympathies seem to lie in the general direction of the Third Force, has freely admitted to discussing in his text, *The Personal World*, subjects that may be considered "unscientific".[19] For an understanding of personality, he says, *"we must recognize the great scope of human experience"*,[20] and he accepts the possibility that human experience may extend beyond the range of scientific observation. He concludes his chapter on telepathy, hallucinatory experiences, and religious ecstasy by noting that those who accept for study only the perception of external reality must reject his discussion; but that others who do not rule out the possibility of "realities beyond the perceiver himself" may treat his discussion "with more respect".[21] What seems most significant is that McCurdy clearly defines the difference between the "post-Newtonian" or scientific view of the world and the "Dantean-New-

[18] *Ibid.*, p. 11.
[19] New York, Harcourt, Brace & World, Inc., 1961, p. 465.
[20] *Ibid.*, p. 464.
[21] *Ibid.*, p. 510.

tonian" view of the world as though modern man could still make a choice.[22]

Ruth Nanda Anshen, describing the purpose of The Credo Series in her introduction to Erich Fromm's book *Beyond the Chains of Illusion*, reveals a general faith in man and also a hope that the Series may "point to a new dimension of morality – not that of constraint and prohibition but a morality that lies as a fountainhead within the human soul, a morality of aspiration to spiritual experience".[23] Miss Anshen hopes that through self-knowledge and work man may "experience a unity of faith, labor and grace which prepares the mind for receiving a truth from sources over which it has no control".[24]

Self-actualization, then, is a process involving preparation and fulfillment through works. It does not imply a state of rest any more than Sanctification, to Mather or Franklin, implied the passive enjoyment of grace. The self-actualized man accepts as a challenge the ultimate of human ironies – that is, that his goals, once reached, will be replaced by new goals. He seeks what is "strictly speaking, unattainable. Propriate striving [i.e., striving toward fulfillment] confers unity upon personality, but it is never the unity of fulfillment, of repose, or of reduced tension." [25] Such striving is inevitable because of that "human predicament presented by the gap between human aspirations and human limitations (between what the human being *is*, what he would *like* to be, and what he *could* be)".[26] It is this same heightened awareness of future possibility that makes Mather mourn his slothfulness and fear that he must leave great things undone; it is this awareness that makes Franklin (though with less feeling of personal guilt) chafe at the difference between what he can do and what there is to be done.

Both Mather and Franklin realized that once man's abilities were developed he could accomplish a great deal, but they were

[22]   *Ibid.*, pp. 576-577.
[23]   New York, Pocket Books, Inc., 1963, p. xix.
[24]   *Ibid.*
[25]   Allport, p. 67.
[26]   Maslow, *Toward a Psychology of Being*, p. 10

also aware that man's hopes must outstrip his progress. Nevertheless they chose, as many Americans have regularly chosen since their time, to strive for fulfillment in action and in works, and to hope that the gap between desire and reality might somehow be lessened as men develop what is best in human nature.

BIBLIOGRAPHY

Aldridge, A. O., "Franklin's 'Shaftesburian' Dialogues not Franklin's: A Revision of the Franklin Canon", *American Literature*, 21 : 151-159 (May, 1949).

Allport, Gordon W., *Becoming* (New Haven, Yale University Press, Sixth printing, 1962).

Anshen, Ruth, "Introduction", Erich Fromm, *Beyond the Chains of Illusion* (New York, Pocket Books, Inc., 1963).

Beall, Otho T., "Cotton Mather's Early 'Curiosa Americana' and the Boston Philosophical Society of 1683", *William and Mary Quarterly*, 18 : 360-372 (July, 1961).

Beall, Otho, Jr., and Shyrock, Richard H., "Cotton Mather: First Significant Figure in American Medicine", *Proceedings of the American Antiquarian Society* (Worcester, Mass., Published by the Society, 1954), v. 63, pp. 37-274.

Becker, Carl L., "Franklin, Benjamin", *Dictionary of American Biography*, ed. by Allen Johnson and Dumas Malone (New York, Charles Scribner's Sons, 1931), v. 6, pp. 585-598.

Benz, Ernest, "Ecumenical Relations between Boston Puritanism and German Pietism: Cotton Mather and August Hermann Francke", *Harvard Theological Review*, 54 : 159-193 (July, 1961).

——, "Pietist and Puritan Sources of Early Protestant World Missions", *Church History*, 20 : 28-55 (1951).

Bingham, H., "Elihu Yale Governor, Collector and Benefactor", *Proceedings of the American Antiquarian Society*, new series (Worcester, Mass., Published by the Society, 1938), v. 47, pp. 93-144.

Boas, Ralph P. and Boas, Louise, *Cotton Mather* (Archon Books, Hamden, Connecticut, reprint 1964).

Boorstin, Daniel J., *The Americans* (New York, Random House, 1958).

Brewster, David, *The Life of Sir Isaac Newton* (London, William Tegg and Co., 1875).

Bruce, William C., *Benjamin Franklin, Self-Revealed* (New York, G. P. Putnam's Sons, 1917).

Calvin, John, *Institutes of the Christian Religion*, translated and collated by John Allen, seventh American Edition, revised and corrected (Philadelphia, Presbyterian Board of Christian Education, n.d.).

Christensen, Merton A., "Franklin on the Hemphill Trial: Deism versus

Presbyterian Orthodoxy", *William and Mary Quarterly*, 10 : 422-440 (1953).

Cohen, I. Bernard, *Franklin and Newton* (Philadelphia, American Philosophical Society, 1956).

Cotton, John, "Christian Calling", *The American Puritans*, ed. by Perry Miller (Garden City, New York, Doubleday Anchor Books, 1956).

Fay, Bernard, *Franklin: The Apostle of Modern Times* (Boston, Little, Brown and Company, 1929).

Ford, Paul L., *The Many-Sided Franklin* (New York, The Century Co., 1899).

Franklin, Benjamin, *The Autobiography*, ed. by Leonard W. Labaree *et al.* (New Haven, Yale University Press, 1964).

——, *The Papers of Benjamin Franklin*, ed. by Leonard W. Labaree *et al.* (New Haven, Yale University Press, 1959-1963), 7 vols.

——, *The Writings of Benjamin Franklin*, ed. by Albert H. Smyth (New York, The Macmillan Company, 1905-1907), 10 vols.

Griswold, A. W., "Three Puritans on Prosperity: Cotton Mather, Benjamin Franklin and Timothy Dwight", *New England Quarterly*, 7 : 475-493 (Summer 1934).

Hale, E. E., "What Made Benjamin Franklin?", *Christian Examiner*, 66 : 265-274 (March, 1859).

Herbert, Edward, Lord of Cherbury, *De Religione Laici*, ed. and tr. by Harold R. Hutcheson (New Haven, Yale University Press, 1944).

Hofstadter, Richard, *Anti-intellectualism in American Life* (New York, Alfred A. Knopf, 1963).

Holmes, Thomas James, *Cotton Mather: A Bibliography of His Works* (Cambridge, Harvard University Press, 1940), 3 vols.

Hornberger, Theodore, "Notes on the Christian Philosopher", Thomas J. Holmes, *Cotton Mather: A Bibliography of His Works* (Cambridge, Harvard University Press, 1940), v. 1, pp. 133-138.

Kittredge, George L., "Notes on Witchcraft", *Proceedings of the American Antiquarian Society* (Worcester, Mass., Published by the Society, 1907), v. 18, pp. 148-212.

Labaree, Leonard W. *et al.*, "Introduction", Benjamin Franklin, *The Autobiography* (New Haven, Yale University Press, 1964).

Larrabee, Harold A., "Poor Richard in an Age of Plenty", *Harper's*, 212 : 64-68 (January, 1956).

McCurdy, Harold Grier, *The Personal World* (New York, Harcourt, Brace & World, Inc., 1961).

Maslow, Abraham H., "A Theory of Human Motivation", *Psychological Review*, 50 : 370-396 (1943).

——, *Toward a Psychology of Being* (Princeton, D. Van Nostrand Company, Inc., 1962).

Mather, Cotton, *Bonifacius: An Essay Upon the Good that is to be Devised and Designed, by Those Who Desire to Answer the Great End of Life, and to Do Good While They Live* (Boston, printed by B. Green, 1710), microcard copy.

——, *Christian Philosopher* (Charlestown, 1815), microfilm copy.

——, *Diary of Cotton Mather*, ed. by Worthington Chauncey Ford, *Massa-*

chusetts Historical Society Collections, seventh Series (Boston, Published by the Society, 1911), vols. 7 and 8.

——, *The Diary of Cotton Mather, D. D., F. R. S. for the Year 1712*, ed. by William R. Manierre (Charlottesville, Va., The University Press of Virginia, 1964), II.

——, *Manuductio ad Ministerium. Directions for a Candidate of the Ministry* (Boston, 1726). Microfilm copy.

——, *Mather Papers*, Notes by Rev. Thomas Prince, ed. by C. Robbins, H. W. Torrey, and S. K. Lothrop, *Massachusetts Historical Society Collections* (Boston, Published by the Society, 1868), v. 8, pp. 383-462.

——, *The Wonders of the Invisible World* (Mount Vernon, New York, The Peter Pauper Press, n.d.).

Mather, Samuel, *The Life of the Very Reverend and Learned Cotton Mather* ... (Boston, 1729), the title page is not the original one, but a later typewritten insertion.

Miller, Perry, *The New England Mind from Colony to Province* (Cambridge, Harvard University Press, 1953).

——, *The New England Mind: The Seventeenth Century* (Cambridge, Harvard University Press, 1954).

More, Paul E., *Benjamin Franklin* (Boston, Houghton Mifflin Company, 1900).

Morison, Samuel Eliot, *The Puritan Pronoas* (New York, New York University Press, 1936).

Murdock, Kenneth B., "Cotton Mather and the Rectorship of Yale College", *Publications of the Colonial Society of Massachusetts* (Boston, Published by the Society, 1927), v. 26, pp. 388-401.

——, *Increase Mather: The Foremost American Puritan* (Cambridge, Harvard University Press, 1925).

——, "Introduction", Cotton Mather, *Selections from Cotton Mather* (New York, Hafner Publishing Company, 1926).

Parrington, Vernon L., *Main Currents in American Thought* (New York, Harcourt, Brace and World, Inc., 1954), v. 1, pp. 107-118, 166-181.

Parton, James, *The Life and Times of Benjamin Franklin* (New York, Mason Brothers, 1864), 2 vols.

Peabody, William B. O., "Life of Cotton Mather", *The Library of American Biography*, ed. by Jared Sparks (Boston, Hilliard, Gray, and Company, 1836), v. 6, pp. 163-350.

Perry, Ralph Barton, *Characteristically American* (New York, Alfred A. Knopf, 1949).

Riley, I. Woodbridge, *American Philosophy* (New York, Russell and Russell, n.d.).

Ross, John, "The Character of Poor Richard: Its Source and Alteration", *Publication of the Modern Language Association*, 55 : 785-794 (September, 1940).

Savelle, Max, *Seeds of Liberty* (New York, A. A. Knopf, 1948).

Shipton, Clifford K., "The New England Clergy", *Publications of the Colonial Society of Massachusetts* (Boston, Published by the Society, 1937), v. 32, pp. 24-54.

Tawney, R. H., *Religion and the Rise of Capitalism* (New York, Harcourt, Brace and Company, 1926).

Van Doren, Carl, *Benjamin Franklin* (New York, The Viking Press, 1938).

Wigglesworth, Michael, *The Day of Doom* (New York, American News Company, 1867).

STUDIES IN AMERICAN LITERATURE

1. JOHN BERNSTEIN: *Pacifism and Rebellion in the Writings of Herman Melville.* 1964. 232 pp.   *f* 25.—

2. KARL F. KNIGHT: *The Poetry of John Crowe Ransom: A Study of Diction, Metaphor, and Symbol.* 1964. 133 pp.   *f* 14.50

3. KENT G. GALLAGHER: *The Foreigner in Early American Drama.* A Study in Attitudes. 1966. 206 pp., Cloth.   *f* 24.—

4. PAUL T. NOLAN: *Three Plays by J. W. (Capt. Jack) Crawford: An Experiment in Myth-Making.* 1966. 287 pp., portrait.   *f* 30.—

5. NORMAN J. FEDDER: *The Influence of D. H. Lawrence on Tennessee Williams.* 1966. 131 pp. Cloth.   *f* 18.—

6. LEONARD GREENBAUM: *The Hound & Horn: The History of a Literary Quarterly.* 1966. 275 pp. 2 plates.   *f* 30.—

7. KENNETH E. RICHARDSON: *Force and Faith in the Novels of William Faulkner.* 1967. 187 pp.   *f* 23.—

10. EDWARD M. HOLMES: *Faulkner's Twice-Told Tales: His Re-Use of His Material.* 1966. 118 pp.   *f* 19.—

16. JOHN D. BRANTLEY: *The Fiction of John Dos Passos.* 1967. 156 pp.   *f* 21.—

17. GEORGE BRANDON SAUL: *Quintet: Essays on Five American Poets.* 1967. 50 pp.   *f* 10.—

MOUTON · PUBLISHERS · THE HAGUE